W9-BVA-418

Connecting Standards and Assessment through Literacy

Connecting Standards and Assessment through Literacy

Mark W. Conley
Michigan State University

BISHOP MUELLER LIBRARY
Briar Cliff University
SIOUX CITY, IA 51104

PEARSON

Boston ■ New York ■ San Francisco
Mexico City ■ Montreal ■ Toronto ■ London ■ Madrid ■ Munich ■ Paris
Hong Kong ■ Singapore ■ Tokyo ■ Cape Town ■ Sydney

Senior Series Editor: *Aurora Martínez Ramos*
Editorial Assistant: *Kevin Shannon*
Senior Marketing Manager: *Krista Groshong*
Composition and Prepress Buyer: *Linda Cox*
Manufacturing Buyer: *Andrew Turso*
Cover Administrator: *Joel Gendron*
Editorial-Production Service: *Matrix Productions Inc.*
Illustrations: *Omegatype Typography, Inc.*
Electronic Composition: *Omegatype Typography, Inc.*

For related titles and support materials, visit our online catalog at www.ablongman.com.

Copyright © 2005 Pearson Education, Inc.

All rights reserved. No part of the material protected by this copyright notice may be reproduced or utilized in any form or by any means, electronic or mechanical, including photocopying, recording, or by any information storage and retrieval system, without written permission of the copyright owner.

To obtain permission(s) to use material from this work, please submit a written request to Allyn and Bacon, Permissions Department, 75 Arlington Street, Boston, MA 02116 or fax your request to 617-848-7320.

Between the time Website information is gathered and then published, it is not unusual for some sites to have closed. Also, the transcription of URLs can result in unintended typographical errors. The publisher would appreciate notification where these errors occur so that they may be corrected in subsequent editions.

Library of Congress Cataloging-in-Publication Data

Conley, Mark William.
    Connecting standards and assessment through literacy / Mark W. Conley.
        p. cm.
    Includes bibliographical references and index.
    ISBN 0-205-35133-6
        1. Education—Standards—United States.   2. Educational tests and measurements—United States.   3. Content area reading—United States.   4. Test-taking skills—United States.   I. Title.

LB3060.83.C65 2005   *BK*
379.1'58—dc22   *$ 32.40*

                                                                      2004052994

Printed in the United States of America

10 9 8 7 6 5 4 3 2   09 08 07 06 05

55948237

To my Dad, the tool and die maker

We went out to his shop in the garage, where he took me on a tour of his toolbox. He showed me all of the parts and gadgets he made. Some were parts of the Apollo moon rockets. He told me how he could see the finished metal in 3-D, in his head, even before he turned on the machines.

"That's like when I write," I explained. "I can see the big chunks in my head."

He just smiled.

CONTENTS

PREFACE

Like many others, I didn't plan to go into assessment; it found me, in 1985, when I was asked to join a committee charged with designing the framework and item specifications for our state's proficiency examination. Ever since then, I have been immersed in assessment, particularly around literacy, but also in the ways in which literacy and specialized uses of language pervade assessment in all subject areas, including English, mathematics, science, and social studies. I wrote this book to share what I have learned from working with many national and state education officials and curriculum specialists, school administrators, dedicated teachers, and their students.

The book is organized into three sections. The first section, "High Standards and High-Stakes Assessment: The Literacy Connection," provides an overview of what it means to have higher educational standards combined with high-stakes assessment. This section covers the history of the standards and high-stakes assessment movements, as well as their modern implications.

The second section, "Connecting Standards, Assessment, and Daily Practice," offers detailed guidance for clarifying and communicating the meaning behind standards and tests and for translating understandings of standards and tests into classroom practices. A highlight of this section is a chapter on how to see connections across standards and tests in order to integrate knowledge about standards and tests smoothly into teaching and learning. A chapter about promoting reading fluency is also included in this section. Fluency is a concern especially for early literacy, prevention of reading failure, and intervention on behalf of adolescent struggling readers. It is a concern highlighted by **No Child Left Behind,** the federal initiative to improve literacy nationwide.

The third section, "Connecting Classroom Practice to Student Achievement," focuses on how to use, gather, and communicate assessment information responsibly so that children will be able to reach greater levels of achievement. This section contains chapters on how to make sense of large-scale assessment information; how to select, design, and implement classroom assessments; and how to communicate assessment information from classroom to classroom, school to school, and even district to district.

I would like to thank Karen Wixson and Charlie Peters for their ideas about state assessment; Bill and Fran Mester for helping me think about outcomes for kids; Rick Stiggins, whose work inspired me to think more deeply about assessment, especially keeping students at the center; Laura Roehler for reminding me that assessment is about growth *and* achievement; Sheila Potter for her expertise in translating assessment policy into practice; and my fellow flight instructors at Lansing Community College for helping me sharpen my thinking about standards and assessment. I would also like to thank the reviewers of this book: Jeanne B. Cobb, Eastern New Mexico University; Virginia C. Hamm, Athens State

University; and Kathy Hawks, Concord College. Special thanks to my children, Kelly and Erin, who keep asking if I'm writing another book and will they be in it (here you are)! And finally, thanks to my wife, Tami. Whenever I wonder whether I should take on a new challenge, from writing a book to biking across Iowa or playing a Stratocaster, I can always count on her to say, "Go for it!"

Mark Conley
East Lansing, Michigan

FOREWORD

In our professional development work at the Assessment Training Institute, we operate on the belief that practitioners can learn to apply sound assessment practices most effectively when they approach the topic with a specific context in mind. That is, the question *"How* should I assess?" can be addressed intelligently only after having answered the questions *"Why* assess?" and "Assess *what?"* The strength of this text by Mark Conley is that he contextualizes his treatment of sound assessment practices in just this manner. He urges that we assess in the literacy context only when we are clear about (1) whom we are trying to help with assessment results and (2) the nature of the achievement standards to be assessed.

Over the past four decades, we have been experiencing a slow but steady transformation of the mission of schools in our society. Dr. Conley's clear and explicit treatment of assessment in standards-based learning environments is further evidence of the completion of this transformation.

Gradually, over the past 40 years, schools that had previously been assigned the mission of producing a dependable rank order of students according to their achievement at the end of high school have been given the assignment of helping all students become competent readers, writers, and math problem solvers. This transformation is driven, I believe, by the realization that if all schools do is sort students just before graduation, then the bottom third to half of that distribution (along with all who dropped out before graduation time!) fail to develop the foundational competencies in reading, writing, and math problem solving that they need to survive in an increasingly complex society.

This transformation has its pedagogical roots in the work of Professor Ben Bloom and his associates at the University of Chicago in the 1960s and 1970s with Bloom's conceptualization of mastery learning classrooms. Schools would seek competence, not merely a rank order. The first practical manifestation of this vision was the behavioral objectives movement of the 1970s, followed by the minimum competencies movement and then by outcomes-based education in the 1980s—all held proficiency-based expectations of students. Each new iteration commanded greater respect in the schooling process than the one that preceded it, but ultimately each fell prey to its own important weaknesses. As time passed, however, society and our school culture kept returning to this vision of mastery learning schools. We found ways to overcome the weaknesses of each failed manifestation of the vision so that its evolution could continue. Thus we have arrived today at the latest version of the mastery learning concept: standards-based schools. After decades of trial and trouble, we have embraced the view that mastery learning will drive the development of effective schools.

This sets the stage for Dr. Conley's treatment of assessment in standards-based schools. The problem he addresses is that the evolution described above has forced us to confront a critical assessment issue: Assessment, evaluation, and grading practices born and bred to produce dependable rankings—that is, to help only a few students succeed—must now be transformed into practices that permit *all* students to succeed. Over the past 40 years, this shift in the assessment paradigm has shaken the measurement community to its foundation. This book helps practitioners grasp the complexity that has characterized this facet of the evolution of schools.

Over the past decade, we have experienced yet another kind of evolution in our thinking about effective assessment. We have come to understand that in addition to using assessment to document or verify student learning, we can use the assessment process and its results as instruction and as a motivator encouraging students to learn more. In our work at the Assessment Training Institute, we refer to this as the distinction between assessment *of learning* and assessment *for learning*. Moreover, we believe that both are important—that they must be in balance if assessment is to help us develop effective schools. We must find and exploit the synergy between them to promote student well-being. In this book, Dr. Conley maps a clear route to balance between the use of large-scale assessment to serve its intended purposes and the use of classroom assessment to meet the information needs of its intended users.

Without question, the most important—and most visible—form of achievement in the United States today is the development of reading proficiencies. Dr. Conley outlines the nature of those proficiencies and the reasons for their prominence. Further, the dimension of pedagogy that is commanding the most attention in our professional circles at all levels these days is assessment practices. In this volume, Professor Conley has presented the most current sense of best practices in assessment. He pools the collective wisdom of his colleagues from across the nation and then adds his own insights and practical suggestions to that vision of excellence in assessment. In these tumultuous times of rapidly evolving schools and politically volatile issues, such a commonsense approach to this complex set of assessment challenges is much needed.

Rick Stiggins
Assessment Training Institute
Portland, Oregon

ABOUT THE AUTHOR

Dr. Mark Conley is an associate professor of teacher education at Michigan State University, where he teaches undergraduate and graduate courses in content area literacy, action research, and assessment. His research and teaching interests focus on content area literacy at the middle and high school levels, classroom literacy assessment, literacy policy, and school-university collaboration. He has consulted with the Michigan Department of Education as well as many schools and school districts on standards and assessment issues and practices.

He also coordinates and teaches the field-based content area literacy course for undergraduate secondary teacher preparation students. In this course, over 250 students are prepared for tutoring middle school adolescents in urban schools. In addition, he designs online courses in content area literacy, classroom assessment, and action research.

In his spare time, he is a flight instructor, plays and custom-builds handmade guitars, and is a long-distance bicyclist. He lives with his wife and daughters in East Lansing, Michigan.

Connecting Standards and Assessment through Literacy

High Standards and High-Stakes Assessment: The Literacy Connection

CHAPTER

1 Higher Educational Standards

This chapter defines standards at different levels of schooling, their impact in the classroom, and the potential of standards for changing curriculum and assessment.

THE WORLD IN REVIEW

*There was excitement in Mrs. Boyd's third grade classroom as the students made their final preparations for their **World in Review** project presentations. The assignment: Research a country somewhere in the world, including the climate and natural resources, the history and government, and how people live and make a living there. Mrs. Boyd had launched the project nearly three weeks earlier, handing out an outline for the project and explaining her expectations. Then, she and the students discussed the quality of the work that needed to go into the project. She asked students, "If you do really well on this, what will your project look like?" The students came up with a number of options for the presentations, including artwork, poster presentations, graphs, and charts. They also talked about how the presentations would be evaluated. Together, Mrs. Boyd and her students put together a simple rubric that they would use to critique the projects. The students would use the rubric to evaluate their own projects. Then Mrs. Boyd would use the rubric to weigh in with her evaluation.*

Each student was encouraged to work with a parent, grandparent, or older sibling. Class days were spent learning skills required for the unit, including how to select a country, use research skills, take notes, and do the writing for the project. As the presentation day approached, Mrs. Boyd and her students discussed specifics about how the presentations would be conducted. Some students struggled with boiling down all of their information into conclusions. Mrs. Boyd noted any struggles and taught skills as needed. She was also able to pair students up to help one another. Parents were invited to be part of the project presentation. Mrs. Boyd and her students prepared a program for the big day.

*The **World in Review** presentations celebrated the students' hard work. Students beamed as they explained the nuances of life in countries that, three weeks ago, were*

3

totally unknown to them. Kelly talked about Thailand, explaining that she chose that country because her father needed to go there as part of his job. Jason's project focused on Transylvania, a place he had always wanted to visit because of Count Dracula. Louis exhibited his posters depicting ways of life in Brazil, his grandparents' ancestral home. Tia and Keisha teamed to explore two different countries in Africa. Their collages showed the vast differences in climate and lifestyle across the African continent. At the conclusion of the presentations, the class adjourned for a light international meal, provided by students and their parents representing the many different ethnic groups within Mrs. Boyd's class.

*Mrs. Boyd reflected on the outcomes of the **World in Review** unit. The unit did an excellent job of helping students meet many of the state and district standards. The students used inquiry to develop historical, geographical, and civic perspectives on countries around the world, a key social studies objective. The students supported their points of view with evidence uncovered during their research, a skill emphasized on the state proficiency exams. In both conversation and presentation, Mrs. Boyd's students demonstrated that they could compare what they understood about their own country with other countries in the international community.*

What Do Standards Mean for You and Your Students?

Experienced teachers such as Mrs. Boyd often know very well what they are trying to accomplish with their students. But long before the modern standards movement, good teachers worked hard to zero in on what students should be able to know and do as a result of their teaching. Knowing and articulating expectations for learning in advance produces all sorts of advantages. Mrs. Boyd, for instance, contemplated well ahead of time what students would accomplish in the *World in Review* unit. She carefully considered national, state, and district standards as she designed activities that fleshed out the unit. Knowing what she and the students were trying to accomplish helped Mrs. Boyd communicate clearly with students about expectations. She was also able to focus specifically on required skills and activities that would help students achieve. Defining goals and expectations helped Mrs. Boyd to anticipate difficulties her students might have and to focus on special kinds of help they might need. Mrs. Boyd and her students had many conversations about the goals, activities, and products of the unit, all guided by explicit understandings of the standards for learning. At the same time, students were able to engage in lots of spontaneous and creative learning, because clear expectations created a structure for them in which they could work productively.

Why Higher Educational Standards?

The movement toward higher educational standards has overtaken all fifty states. This movement was ignited by such blue-ribbon panel publications as *A Nation at Risk* (National Commission on Excellence in Education 1983), *Becoming a Nation of Readers* (Anderson, Hiebert et al. 1985), *Highlights from the Third International Mathematics and Science (TIMMS) Study* (National Center for Education Statistics 1999), *Preventing Reading Difficulties in Young Children* (Snow, Burns et al. 1998), *Report of the National Reading Panel* (National Reading Panel 2000) and, more recently, *Our Schools and Our Future: Are We Still at Risk?* (Peterson 2003). These reports in themselves were initiated by a rash of bad news, including stagnant or declining national test scores as well as international comparisons revealing that American children do poorly—particularly in science and mathematics—when compared with other children around the world. The business community had also voiced concern about the capacity of schools to prepare highly skilled workers.

In the wake of these concerns, policymakers, politicians, and educators have worked diligently to develop and implement more rigorous standards at both the national and state levels. Recently, the federal government authorized legislation under the title **No Child Left Behind (NCLB)** (Bush 2001). This legislation provides for historic and sweeping reforms of schools, including teaching, learning, and assessment practices. States have responded to this legislation with greater scrutiny of school and teacher performance and increased assessment. These reforms are focused especially on students who traditionally have failed to succeed.

An **educational standard** is a statement that depicts what students should know or be able to do as a result of teaching and learning. Some standards are expressed in terms of knowledge or performance in a content area. For instance, a much-discussed general standard for reading is that *all children should be able to read by the end of grade 3.* Another content area standard is that *by the end of grade 3, all children should be able to add, subtract, multiply, and divide whole numbers.* Standards are often written to express different kinds of performance at earlier and later ages or grade levels. For example, first graders, focusing on basic statistical skills, might be held to a standard of accurately counting data. The standard for high school students might require comparisons among different ways of representing data, such as bar charts or line graphs. A more detailed discussion of different types of standards—and how to translate them and transform them into classroom practice—appears in Chapter 3.

What Do Standards Mean for Your School?

Educators have long valued the ability to employ multiple approaches to curricula and teaching. As one walks through the classrooms of many school buildings, this value is apparant in an intriguing abundance of instructional activities. To many, this variety represents creative teaching at it best and diverse students engaged in multiple ways. But without clearly articulated standards, variety can seem confusing and counterproductive to some—such as parents and others whom schools serve. Consider this example.

In one elementary school, three fifth grade teachers approached the reading curriculum in three different ways: One teacher focused on the use of nature in fiction, another did an author study based on Gary Paulson's books, and the third made use of a single chapter book. Despite these differences in approach, all three teachers had the same overarching goal: to help students understand the theme of man versus nature in narratives.

For their part, parents talked with one another and compared notes based on past students' experiences. Across the back fence, neighbors discovered that there were vast differences in the numbers of books students were required to read in these classrooms. The teacher emphasizing nature fiction required four books. The second teacher's author study involved two of Gary Paulson's books: *Hatchet* and *Dogsong*. The third teacher asked students to read a single book, Jean Craighead George's *Julie and the Wolves*.

In the absence of any other information, parents were divided about which approach was best. Some argued that it was better for kids to read lots of books. Some said it was good for kids to get to know one author in depth. Others claimed that the third teacher was able to do a lot using just one book. Each year the school office was inundated with phone calls from parents asking questions about the curriculum, what the teachers were doing and what students in those classrooms were learning. The sixth grade teachers were similarly mystified about what their colleagues were doing and, more important, were puzzled about how to build on their work.

A school-wide focus on standards could help reduce these problems. Buildings that emphasize standards are able to connect multiple teaching approaches to common goals. Teachers in standards-inspired buildings are able to explain to parents how the approach they are taking will help students learn with respect to a set of standards. Teachers from grade to grade are in a good position to build upon past learning because much is known about what is taught and learned each year. Parents feel that they are "in the loop" and can make good choices for their children because they can see connections between the diverse classroom events and goals held in common. Standards make it possible for schools to hum with varied activity in the context of shared knowledge about where teachers and students are going.

What Do Standards Mean for Your School District?

Local school districts must be accountable to the communities they serve. Parents want to know that their local schools are preparing their children to meet the highest standards of achievement. Businesses, churches, and other community stakeholders also rely on school districts to be their best so that the community will thrive. Thus, it is critically important for school districts to be able to explain how they and their students are doing.

Clearly stated standards, used wisely, provide a vehicle for giving a district a reality check. Without clear standards, there can be lots of activity throughout a school district and yet no way of saying consistently or fairly what goals are being met. Without standards, there is no way to select appropriate means to measure or assess how a district is doing. Again, without standards, it is difficult to tell what a district needs, what programs should be developed, and how to address any weaknesses in instruction or assessment. Finally, the absence of standards makes it nearly impossible for a district to communicate the impact or value of monies spent or programs delivered.

Educators need to work hard to ensure that standards—and how they are represented in the classroom—are clearly communicated. Standards can be an effective tool for helping districts reflect, self-evaluate, improve, and create new directions. Standards help school districts unambiguously demonstrate their accountability to the communities they serve.

Three Questions Parents Often Ask:

1. What are you trying to accomplish with my child?
2. How is my child doing?
3. What are you doing to help my child do better?

What Do Standards Mean for Parents?

Often, when parents come in for parent conferences, they have three questions in mind. The first is: "What are you trying to accomplish with my child?" This is a question about standards. It's a way of asking about goals and expectations. A second question is more specific: "How is my child doing?" This question arises from a parent's need to know how well his or her child is meeting expectations. A third question is "What are you doing to help my child do better?" The reasons why a parent might ask this question are many, from trying to determine what is actually happening in the classroom to seeking insight into how the parent might help his or her child.

Parents feel anxiety when teachers are unable or unwilling to answer these questions. The source of this anxiety is easy to understand. Parents want the best for their kids. Uncertainty over goals and progress makes it difficult for parents to see how their child can be successful. More important, parents want to see that their child continually does better. If it is not clear how to do better in a class, it is impossible to tell how to direct motivation and effort to be successful. It is difficult at best for anyone to work hard in the face of murky goals and uncertain rewards for persistent yet unfocused effort.

Standards are a start in providing parents with answers to the questions that concern them most. Standards represent the understandings and performance that teachers and their students are shooting for. They are the guidelines by which student performance is assessed. They can be used to tell what alternatives should be used to help students learn better. And they are the building blocks for student success. In Chapter 12, ways to use standards to answer parents' most pressing questions are explained.

How Can Standards Improve Instruction?

There are many debates about how best to use standards as a guide for teaching and learning. Should standards written at the national level or at the state level be used? What about district-level or school-level standards? Can teachers make up their own standards? The answer to all of these questions is yes.

National and state standards often reflect the most recent research and wisdom of the profession. But because they are written at a more general level, often by content specialists, these standards need to be personalized, or reconsidered in terms of local schools and the needs of local children. Additionally, there can be large numbers of standards from which to choose. These factors impose on the classroom teacher the responsibility to reinterpret and carefully select only the most relevant standards in a timely manner to guide instruction. Can teachers create their own standards? Certainly! Using their experience with children and the instructional materials at hand, many teachers set their own goals. However, the emergence of national and state standards offers several advantages.

First, teachers can consult published standards as one more tool in considering what instruction is appropriate for their students. Being able to consult a body of standards reduces the need to start from scratch every time a teacher plans instruction. Second, published standards invite conversation across classrooms, schools, and districts so that all children receive similar opportunities to achieve. Connecting classroom-based goals to goals held in common at state and national levels boosts the chances that all children will grow in clearly defined directions.

How Can Standards Improve
Classroom Assessment?

Assessment works best when it is guided by well-articulated goals. How many times have you faced a test for which you didn't really know what was expected of you? How did you do? As a teacher, have there been times when you've given an assessment for which you weren't really clear with yourself or your students about what was expected of them? How did your students do?

Thinking about standards in advance of instruction and assessment prevents situations in which goals for assessment are not clear and, as a result, students end up not doing very well at all. Thinking about standards in advance can help you forge a good fit between the goals of your assessment and the assessment techniques you choose. Relationships between standards and different types of assessment are explained throughout this book.

To make the best use of standards, assessment needs to be ongoing. Students do best when they have frequent and continuous feedback about what they know and what they haven't yet mastered. Ongoing assessment takes many forms, from continuous observation of students' performance to portfolios, in which teachers and students gather examples of classroom work while considering how students are growing in what they have learned. Ongoing assessment involves employing varied methods for knowing for whether students are "getting it" and whether more or different types of instruction are required. Guided by standards, ongoing assessment offers the best way of determining what and whether students understand and whether or not it is time to move on.

Making Standards Work for You

Published standards, no matter how well designed, are no substitute for your solid judgment, as a teacher, based on knowledge about teaching and a good understanding of your children. Responding to the calls for teaching to higher-level standards will never be as simple as picking up a book of standards, selecting a few, and then "covering" them with your students. Standards-based teaching and assessment requires decision making about what is appropriate for students in different content areas and at various developmental levels, and it requires considering the diversity of children in background, skill, and motivation. Standards-based teaching and assessment means using what you know to design from scratch, select, interpret, reinvent, and apply standards in ways that will lead your students to higher levels of learning. This text was written as a guide in making standards work for you and your students.

SPECIAL PROJECTS

For Beginning Teachers

Obtain from your state a set of curriculum standards in literacy or another content area. Describe a classroom in which the standards are being implemented. What would the teachers and students be doing? What kinds of assessment would be employed to determine what the students were learning?

For Experienced Teachers

Select a set of standards, and consider how you would respond to the following three questions parents always ask.

- What are you trying to accomplish with my child?
- How is my child doing?
- What are you doing to help my child do better?

Share your responses with colleagues. How would you, or how do you, respond to the fourth question that is often asked: "How is my child doing compared with everyone else?" Compare your answers with those of several colleagues.

SUGGESTED READINGS

Cohn, A. (1999). *The schools our children deserve: Moving beyond traditional classrooms and "tougher standards."* Boston: Houghton Mifflin.
Daniels, H., & Hyde, A. (1998). *Best practice: New standards for teaching and learning in America's schools.* Portsmouth, NH: Heinemann.

2 High-Stakes Assessment

This chapter describes the range and impact of high-stakes assessment, from the national level on into the classroom. It also discusses specific purposes for high-stakes assessment (for example, early assessment and intervention at the early elementary level and gatekeeping assessments across the grades).

What's at Stake in High-Stakes Assessment?

These days, assessment seems to have taken over education and educators at all levels. Tests in and of themselves are not inherently *high-stakes* instruments. Tests can be teacher-made, authentic, informal, formal, observational, or standardized. These characteristics of tests are not mutually exclusive. Tests that start out as teacher-made tests may become formal or even standardized over time. To become standardized, a test is subjected to repeated piloting over time, to multiple comparisons of individual and/or group test performance, and to detailed statistical analyses.

The fact that a test is standardized does not make it any less prone to error or misuse. There are numerous examples of problems with standardized and other kinds of tests. Many of these problems emerge because of misconceptions about the purposes for different tests and because of serious errors in the design of tests. One important purpose of tests—and it is an area in which errors or misuse can have particularly dire consequences—involves the idea of **high-stakes assessment.**

The term *high-stakes* refers to how tests are used. In high-stakes assessment, the test results have clearly defined consequences for students. For example, performance on such an assessment may determine whether a student knows enough or is adequately prepared to move on to the next level, such as first grade. High-stakes assessments may be used to help determine whether someone should be endorsed as a successful reader, a high school graduate, or a teacher. High-stakes assessments are also used to grant or deny admission to college or even entrance into a career. Clearly, errors in the design and/or use of tests employed in high-stakes assessment can have devastating consequences.

This chapter is about high-stakes assessment. It begins with a brief history of high-stakes tests, followed by a description of the various ways in which high-stakes tests are used. Next, the dangers of using tests for high-stakes purposes are discussed. Finally, the differences between high-stakes and growth-oriented assessments are described.

High-Stakes Tests: A Brief History

High-stakes tests are often found at the center of crisis. In 1946 the United States Chamber of Commerce called for high-stakes assessment to ensure that schools would do a good job preparing well-qualified workers for the post–World War II era (Fine 1947). During the Cold War of the 1950s and 1960s, international comparisons based on assessment data created a frenzied atmosphere of reform in reading and mathematics. As teachers organized professionally into labor unions in the late 1960s, state governments sought out high-stakes tests to introduce greater accountability into the public school system. This coincided with a number of high-profile court cases in which the parents of semiliterate or illiterate high school graduates sued school districts for not properly educating their children. High-stakes tests were then employed to identify semiliterate and illiterate students in order to ensure that they were more likely to graduate with the appropriate basic skills. More recently, international assessments have created a national anxiety about the preparation of U.S. students in reading, math, and science (National Center for Education Statistics 1999; National Reading Panel 2000).

In short, it is during times of crisis that high-stakes assessments often become the most popular. When international reports indicate substandard performance in literacy, math, and science, high-stakes assessments are used to identify students who need more help. When the public believes that children are leaving various levels of schooling unable to read or compute, high-stakes assessments emerge to identify problems, design interventions, and determine resulting achievement.

Some Purposes of High-Stakes Assessment

High-stakes assessments are pressed into service for a number of purposes and a variety of audiences. One of the most common purposes is accountability: to hold public schools and teachers responsible for student performance. This often takes the form of comparing student performance on tests with the dollars spent on education. The argument is made that increases in funding for schooling should be accompanied by greater student testing and/or by enhanced student performance on tests (Mazzeo 2001).

High-stakes assessments are frequently used to document and reward achievement. When the government or a school agency wants to know how students or doing, or whether or not students or schools are improving, high-stakes assessments come into play. Assessments become high-stakes because of the consequences that accompany performance. Students who demonstrate high achievement are rewarded financially, as in some states that award college funds on the basis of test performance. Schools with high achievement may enjoy greater funding for materials or favorite programs. In some cases, teachers are offered incentives for their students' successful test performance. The reverse is also true; that is, poor performance can lead to negative consequences, such as cuts in funding, fines, teacher and student transfers, and the closing down of schools.

High-stakes assessment is often an integral part of reform and improvement. When national or state assessment data support the idea that schools are doing poorly, politicians use test results to instigate, guide, and monitor reforms. In some cases, this means that a government or school agency takes greater control over what is taught and how learning is assessed. If things are going badly, some will use the results of high-stakes tests to point out the direction for improvement. Others use performance on high-stakes tests to claim that a school, classroom, or individual child has achieved.

A popular misconception is that high-stakes tests take only the form of large-scale, standardized tests. On the contrary, teachers also use a variety of other tests for high-stakes purposes. Section or chapter tests, for instance, are used to monitor progress through literature series, as well as through mathematics, science, and social studies texts. In some schools, performance on these or other published or teacher-constructed content area tests can mean the difference between reteaching a student and allowing him or her to move on to the next level or set of ideas. An accumulation of bad performances on these tests could mean the difference between passing and failing a grade.

The Dangers of High-Stakes Assessment

So what's wrong with this picture? The urgency associated with high-stakes tests and the crises they are designed to solve often leads to ill-conceived, knee-jerk reactions that don't effectively address the original crises.

Consider, for example, discrepancies in test performance that emerge between rich and poor communities. Typically, policymakers create laws and regulations with the intention of reducing the gap in test performance between the rich and the poor. However, when the test scores are bad, the more affluent schools are better able than their impoverished counterparts to apply the funds needed to improve performance. Schools in impoverished communities, on the other hand, are often subjected to penalties, including reductions in funding, as a consequence of poor performance. The end result is that the rich get richer, with higher test scores, while the poor get poorer, with even lower test performance (Allington 2002).

Yet another problem concerns the ways high-stakes test performance is misinterpreted or manipulated for various purposes. For instance, a popular notion has been that America's schools are in crisis because of a decline in SAT scores over a 20-year period. Some researchers have argued that this decline is actually the result of skillful political manipulation of the testing data to increase pressure on public schools to reform and do better. The reality, according to these researchers, is that SAT scores have remained stable for the past 20 years (Berliner 1996). More recently, high-profile national reports have been criticized for selectively interpreting research and high-stakes testing data to create biased prescriptions for early literacy instruction (Allington 2002). Tests used for high-stakes purposes have also been implicated in increased retention rates (holding students back in a grade) for English as a Second Language (ESL) learners and African American students. Students who are held back, especially as they get older, are at increased risk for continued failure or even dropping out of school (Valencia and Wixson 1999).

Researchers have observed that the more a test is used for high-stakes purposes, the greater the chance for distortion in the conclusions and inferences based on the results (Amrein and Berliner 2002). The historical use of high-stakes tests to resolve crises has not been very effective and warrants constant scrutiny. Given the limitations of test interpretations within a high-stakes environment and the likelihood of misuse of results, the role of high-stakes tests within reform must be continuously questioned. Published or teacher-made tests may provide only an inexact measure of what students know and are able to do. But standardized tests too, though commonly perceived as infallible, can suffer their own imperfections in conception, design, and implementation.

Remember this admonition: The more a test is used for high-stakes purposes, the more likely that test is to be misinterpreted and misused, despite potentially life-changing consequences. Educating yourself about various tests—their design, implementation, and interpretation, as well as their use under high-stakes conditions—is the best way to confront and limit the problems inherent in high-stakes testing.

Taking High-Stakes Snapshots versus Observing Growth over Time

Tests used for high-stakes purposes usually offer a snapshot—a one-time assessment of how much a student knows or is able to do. Teachers, parents, school administrators, and policymakers often use high-stakes snapshots to answer the question "How is my child/school/district/state/nation doing?" In comparison **growth-oriented assessments** take the form of multiple assessments, measuring and representing a student's performance (or multiple aspects of a student's performance) over time. Ideally, good assessment should showcase a student's growth *and* achievement—both the journey and the destination—to provide a more comprehensive picture of what a student has achieved and what it took to get there. Taking this approach at the outset makes it possible to understand the full scope of a student's achievement, what happens when roadblocks and detours occur on the way to achievement, and how students can be helped along.

Test used for high-stakes purposes usually offer only a snapshot of achievement.

Tests designed with high-stakes purposes in mind might look very different from tests designed to be growth-oriented assessments. The format and scheduling of high-stakes, snapshot tests are often dictated by considerations of time and expense. Because they are often administered on a large scale (school-, district-, state- or even nationwide) to large groups of students for purposes of assessing achievement and accountability, high-stakes tests tend to consist of multiple-choice or short-answer questions with answer formats that are easily scored. There are usually no more than a few forms of a high-stakes test, because the snapshots are taken only once a year or at designated grade levels.

In contrast, assessments that emphasize growth might consist of many types of curriculum-based, published or even teacher-made classroom assessments. They might involve observations of various kinds of student performance, including oral and written performance. They might be embedded in small- or large-scale, curriculum-based projects. In some cases, more formal tests might be used, including standardized tests in a pretest and posttest fashion, to see just how much students have grown in their learning. Growth-oriented assessment practices emphasize the use of multiple indicators and artifacts, as well as complementary and sometimes contrasting means of revealing growth—how much learning has taken place over time, given where students started, what they knew or didn't know, and how and what they understand now.

> **Growth-oriented assessment involves multiple observations of a student's performance over time.**

There are a number of dilemmas associated with the connections between high-stakes and growth-oriented assessments. One issue concerns the extent to which high-stakes and growth-oriented assessments are consistent or compatible with one another. There are many examples of students, having succeeded on growth-oriented, classroom assessments, only to experience less success or even failure on high-stakes assessments.

For instance, in a mathematics class, students may be more than capable of demonstrating their growth in understanding the concept of area when they are discussing the floor plan for their dream house. Their conversations, their computations, their drawings and other illustrations—all combine to show that they understand the concept far better than when they started the unit. And yet, they may falter when they encounter the multiple-choice questions about area on the high-stakes district or state test. This emphasizes the importance of explicitly helping students relate their understandings to the content and format of the high-stakes test(s).

A second example involves early literacy development. Many high-stakes tests are constructed with grade-level goals in mind, such as testing whether all children can read by grade 3. Growth-oriented assessments focused on early literacy are often concerned with gaining a picture of some of the unique ways in which children grow in their oral language and negotiate the transition to written language. These assessments often involve multiple opportunities for observing children's literacy development. In cases where children are falling behind, these assessments provide indications of when early intervention is required and what needs to be done. Ideally, growth-oriented assessments can be organized as an ongoing guide for preparing students to succeed on high-stakes assessments, even though, at first glance, the assessments may have very different purposes.

Demonstrating how patterns of growth and achievement are connected presents a serious challenge, even when classroom and high-stakes assessments are in agreement with one another. The reality is that classroom and high-stakes assessments can be at odds, and when this occurs, it is very difficult to demonstrate growth and achievement. Chapter 4 takes up these issues as part of the problem of clarifying assessment practices and communicating effectively about them.

There is a tendency for educators and others to favor one side or the other when it comes to high-stakes and growth-oriented assessment practices. For instance, politicians often favor high-stakes tests for accountability purposes. Classroom teachers frequently favor growth-oriented assessments for the detailed information they provide about what and how students are learning. In reality, however, we need both kinds of tests. Rather than choosing sides, it is more important to use tests for both growth-oriented and high-stakes purposes: to provide multiple observations of how students are learning over time *and* to determine accountability.

Teachers, parents, and administrators all have a stake in being able to determine how much students have achieved. And politicians and policymakers can make better-informed decisions if they have a fuller picture of how diverse, individual children grow and learn. The challenge is to create channels of communication so that all of these audiences, invested in education from their own perspectives, can have fruitful conversations about ways to support better teaching and learning. How to create these conversations is the topic of Chapter 12.

Integrating High Standards and Assessment

The most obvious challenge for integrating high educational standards and various kinds of assessment concerns complexity. Just as there are many different types of educational standards, there are many different types of tests and purposes for tests, beyond the high-stakes and growth objectives already discussed.

Tests developed at the national level are not necessarily consistent with those employed at state and local levels. Many state standards are written to reflect general grade-level expectations, whereas national tests might zero in on very specific skills or kinds of content. For example, many state standards include the general requirement that students be able to construct meaning from print; many tests used nationally emphasize specific skills important for early reading fluency, such as alphabetic knowledge, phonemic awareness, and word recognition. Challenges for teachers and their students emerge when states that formerly supported general standards adopt the more specific tests. This situation is occurring in many states where general standards are colliding with the very specific testing expectations for early literacy in No Child Left Behind.

Similarly, there is no guarantee that various tests are in any way in agreement with one another in what they test, how they test, and what they communicate about students' performance. Moreover, standards and assessments of all kinds are not always selected, implemented, or interpreted with the same purposes, audiences, or consequences in mind. There can be considerable disagreement about what standards and assessments actually mean for instructional and assessment practices (Valencia and Wixson 1999).

Educational standards and assessments are often developed quite independently of one another (Valencia and Wixson 1999). Many states, for instance, developed statewide testing in the late 1960s and 1970s but did not get into designing educational standards until the 1990s or later. In many cases, the groups and committees that created the tests are not the same groups that designed the educational standards. Consequently, although there is the superficial impression that educational standards and assessments are congruent, in fact, they are quite likely to imply different things, in terms of directions for instruction and assessment (Mazzeo 2001).

The mandates and consequences for participating in statewide assessment and adopting higher educational standards can also vary (Valencia and Wixson 1999). As a result, the accountability messages that tests and standards communicate can be very different. In some states, accountability with regard to higher educational standards continues to be voluntary, whereas participation in state assessments is most often mandatory. When standards and assessments are on such unequal footing, it can be extremely difficult to mount an integrated effort to implement standards and respond to state tests.

Some states have strived to ensure that standards and assessments are consistent with one another (Valencia and Wixson 1999). Standards and high-stakes assessments that are developed at the same time by like-minded groups of individuals exhibit a great deal more consistency in the messages they send about desired curricula and assessment practices. However, the mere fact that standards and tests appear to be cut from the same cloth is no guarantee that standards and assessments will be easily integrated, especially at the classroom level. Standards and assessments are open to a wide range of interpretation. In addition, there can be considerable gaps between what standards and assessments imply and classroom practice itself. As a result, many teachers, schools, and districts struggle with what it means to be accountable to high standards *and* high-stakes tests.

With this much diversity of political pressure and interpretation in the educational system, what is the true potential for integrating high standards and assessments into effective teaching and learning? One way to answer this question involves figuring out exactly what messages are implied by different standards and assessments (Chapters 3 and 4), selecting targets and strategies based on common understandings (Chapters 5 and 6) and designing lessons that integrate standards and test-taking skills (Chapters 7, 8, and 9). Finally, it is important to make sense of students' growth and achievement while we are learning to communicate how they—and the educational system—are doing (Chapters 10, 11, and 12). These are the themes around which this book is organized.

SPECIAL PROJECTS

For Beginning Teachers

Reports on testing and school performance appear frequently in the media (newspapers, magazines, and television) and on the Internet. Find an article, televised account or website that reports on the results of a test, preferably a high-stakes test. Some of the more commonly reported tests are

- national tests, such as the SAT, ACT tests, and the National Test of Educational Progress
- state competency and proficiency tests
- local school district tests

Examine the article, report, or website for evidence of

- purposes for using the test (such as reform or accountability)
- high-stakes consequences (such as impact on a school, decisions about students—passing, failing, reteaching, retaining, rewarding)

Now examine the article, report, or website for evidence of

- misuse or misinterpretation of a test or the data it yields
- problems with communicating results and/or with fairness

Finally, explain whether you think the use of this test is or is not appropriate, given the test itself, its interpretation, and its use for high-stakes purposes. Are there better ways in which the same purposes could be accomplished? Would looking at growth and achievement be more appropriate, or not?

For Experienced Teachers

1. What kinds of tests are emphasized in your school? Talk to administrators, colleagues, and parents, and ask the following questions:

- Which tests are the most important? Why?
- What do you value in a good test?
- What information should a good test provide?

2. Select an area of assessment (such as literacy, mathematics, science, or social studies). Select two tests in the area, one that is used to assess high-stakes achievement and another that is used to assess growth. In what ways are these tests similar? In what ways are they different? Consider their format, the ways in which they are used, what they communicate, and their intended audiences.

3. Select a test with which you are familiar. Now select a related set of educational standards. For example, if you select an early reading test, select a set of early reading standards. Examine the test and the standards for common points. To what extent are the test and standards in agreement with one another? In what ways are they different?

SUGGESTED READINGS

Tierney, R. (1999). Literacy assessment reform: Shifting beliefs, principled possibilities, and emerging practices. In S. Berrentine (Ed.), *Reading assessment: Principles and practices for elementary teachers*, pp. 10–29. Newark, DE: International Reading Association.

Wiggins, G. (1999). *Assessing student performance: Exploring the purpose and limits of testing.* New York: Wiley.

Connecting Standards, Assessment, and Daily Practice

3 Clarifying and Communicating about Standards

This chapter portrays a process for converting standards into simpler language, committing to a small number of standards, and then having conversations about standards across the curriculum.

What Kinds of Standards?

In this era of pushing for higher levels of achievement, there are many different kinds of standards. Unfortunately, many standards are written in edu-speak—that is, language that may be somewhat intelligible to educators but incomprehensible to those with whom we work, such as our students, parents, and others concerned about education. And even when standards are relatively straightforward, there may be little agreement about what they mean or how they should be enacted.

This chapter details the more popular types of standards and then discusses some ways to translate them into more accessible language. Next, the chapter describes how to commit to a few standards and thus pave the way for productive conversations about what standards mean and how they look in various classrooms.

Developmental Standards

Developmental standards focus on the phases or levels of development that individual children exhibit. Authors of developmental standards strive to capture sequences of growth and change that occur in children. These standards are often expressed in terms of *age appropriateness;* they reflect the development of children within a particular age span. They are also constructed with *individual appropriateness* in mind; they reflect the fact that each child is unique in personality traits, learning style, and family background. One purpose of developmental standards is to help teachers and other caregivers prepare behaviors, activities, and materials appropriate to help each child grow, given what is known about a particular age span and individual. A simple set of developmental standards, focusing on the development of knowledge about the alphabetic, appears in Figure 3.1.

FIGURE 3.1   Sample Developmental Standards in Reading and Writing

Standard: Knows the names of the letters of the alphabet and can identify them in any context.

Level 1. Can recognize a few (5–10) letters, most of them uppercase.

Level 2. Can recognize the majority of the most frequently occurring uppercase and some of the most frequently occurring lowercase letters.

Level 3. Can recognize all of the most frequently occurring upper- and lowercase letters, but not all of the letters.

Level 4. Can recognize all upper- and lowercase letters.

Source: McRel (Bodrova, Leong et al. 2000).

Grade-Level Standards

Another type of standard is a **grade-level standard.** Grade-specific standards specify desirable behaviors as outcomes of a particular grade or a particular unit of study within a grade level. Grade-specific standards may or may not be the product of thinking about children's development. For instance, it has been popular recently for politicians and policymakers to say that every child will be a reader by the end of grade 3. As a result, some authors of these standards begin with grade 3 successful reading as a target and then work back to the desirable early literacy behaviors that will lead up to successful reading by grade 3.

Figure 3.2 depicts a set of grade-level standards for first grade and third grade reading. Note that the first grade standards are simpler than the third grade standards. Note also that the first grade standards could be viewed as building blocks for the more complex third grade standards. In the sense that these standards depict different levels of complexity, the grade-level standards resemble developmental standards. However, grade-level standards can be written entirely without concern for age appropriateness or individual appropriateness. In fact, a criticism of grade-level standards has been that these standards often do not reflect children's growth in realistic ways, especially when they are used to guide the design of grade-level assessments (Ohanian 1999).

Content-Specific Standards

Content-specific standards delineate desired outcomes for subject areas or for concepts within subject areas. Like grade-level standards, content-specific standards may or may not be designed with children's development in mind. Often these standards are used to guide curriculum and assessment decisions, providing targets at different grade-levels, for example.

Not all students necessarily achieve, nor are they always required to achieve, on all of the content-specific targets, and they do not reach these targets at the

FIGURE 3.2 Grade-Level Standards from the Florida Sunshine State Standards

Grade 1 Reading	Grade 3 Reading
■ reads aloud familiar stories, poems, and passages. ■ knows the main idea or theme and supporting details of a story or informational piece. ■ uses specific details and information from a text to answer literal questions. ■ selects material to read for pleasure (for example, favorite books and stories). ■ identifies similarities and differences between two texts (for example, in topics, characters, problems). ■ uses simple reference material to obtain information (for example, table of contents, fiction and nonfiction books, picture dictionaries, audio visual software).	■ constructs meaning from a wide range of texts. ■ reads text and determines the main idea or essential message, identifies relevant supporting details and facts, and arranges events in chronological order. ■ reads and organizes information for a variety of purposes, including making a report, conducting interviews, taking a test, and performing an authentic task. ■ identifies specific personal preferences relative to fiction and nonfiction reading. ■ recognizes the use of comparison and contrast in a text. ■ selects and uses a variety of appropriate reference materials, including multiple representations of information, such as maps, charts, and photos, to gather information for research projects.

same time. Still, content-specific standards serve as useful guideposts for teaching and assessment decisions within many subject areas.

Figure 3.3 depicts content-specific standards for communication arts, and Figure 3.4 shows content-specific standards for science. Note that each set of standards reflects knowledge and tasks deemed unique to and essential for each subject area.

Performance Standards

Performance standards are used to describe desirable outcomes for student skills—in other words, what students should be able to do. For instance, some performance standards depict expectations for students' reading and/or mathematics proficiency: *All elementary and middle school children will read independently and use math to solve problems appropriately at each grade level.* No Child Left Behind legislation mandates a performance standard termed **Adequate Yearly Progress.** Under this provision, each state sets minimum performance levels for students for each year in districts and schools (an example appears in Figure 3.5). Implicit in the provision for Adequate Yearly Progress is the performance standard that *all students will experience a year of academic growth for each year of instruction.*

FIGURE 3.3   Grade-Level Standards for K–12 from the Michigan Standards for Communication Arts

Communication Arts

A literate individual:

- communicates skillfully and effectively through printed, visual, auditory, and technological media in the home, school, community, and workplace;
- thinks analytically and creatively about important themes, concepts, and ideas;
- uses the English language arts to identify and solve problems;
- uses the English language arts to understand and appreciate the commonalities and differences within social, cultural, and linguistic communities;
- understands and appreciates the aesthetic elements of oral, visual, and written texts;
- uses the English language arts to develop insights about human experiences;
- uses the English language arts to develop the characteristics of lifelong learners and workers, such as curiosity, persistence, flexibility, and reflection; and
- connects knowledge from all curriculum areas to enhance understanding of the world.

FIGURE 3.4   Grade-Level Standards for K–12 from the Texas Essential Knowledge and Skills for Science

Science

The student distinguishes between living organisms and nonliving objects.
The student is expected to:

- group living organisms and nonliving objects; and
- compare living organisms and nonliving objects.

The student knows that living organisms have basic needs.
The student is expected to:

- identify characteristics of living organisms that allow their basic needs to be met; and
- compare and give examples of the ways living organisms depend on each other for their basic needs.

The student knows that the natural world includes rocks, soil, and water.
The student is expected to:

- identify and describe a variety of natural sources of water including streams, lakes, and oceans;
- observe and describe differences in rocks and soil samples; and
- identify how rocks, soil, and water are used and how they can be recycled.

FIGURE 3.5   Texas Plan for Adequate Yearly Progress

Adequate Yearly Progress

"Under the provisions in the No Child Left Behind (NCLB) Act, all public school campuses, school districts, and the state are evaluated for Adequate Yearly Progress (AYP). Districts, campuses, and the state are required to meet AYP criteria on three measures—Reading/Language Arts, Mathematics, and either Graduation Rate (for high schools and districts) or Attendance Rate (for elementary and middle/junior high schools)."

Corrective Action

"If a campus, district, or state that is receiving Title I, Part A funds fails to meet AYP for two consecutive years, that campus, district, or state is subject to certain requirements such as offering supplemental education services, offering school choice, and/or taking corrective actions."

Performance standards are thus used to judge not only the performance of students but also that of schools and districts. There are usually incentives designed to encourage success and penalties exacted as a consequence of failure to meet performance standards. These may range from increasing or decreasing funds to rewarding or replacing administrators and teachers and even to closing down entire schools. Compared with other standards described so far, performance standards are sometimes associated with the most far-reaching consequences, good or ill, for students and educational institutions.

Working with Standards

Now that you are familiar with the different types of standards, let's look at some ways to work with standards and prioritize instruction so that they will be useful.

Translate Standards into Plain English

As you have probably experienced, and as the examples presented thus far illustrate, standards documents are not always written with the layperson in mind. They can be full of educational jargon familiar only to those who wrote the standards and to those within the educational community for whom they were written. This is not a problem if you are a member of that select group. However, you may be at a disadvantage if you are a teacher who does not completely understand the standards or know exactly how to interpret them. Imagine the problems posed by standards that are unintelligible to parents and their children. How are these key individuals supposed to know, through the standards alone, about the learning goals that guide what is happening in the school? Because standards can affect all areas of teaching and assessment, it is vital that parents, students, and educators comprehend the standards and be able to communicate about them.

Consequently, standards must be made accessible to all. One way to do this is to translate standards into plain English. An exercise that you may wish to try involves boiling down standards, one at a time, into language that the average person in a shopping mall could understand. Better yet, consider the question so often asked during parent–teacher conferences: "What's new in your classroom this year?" Experiment with restating standards in ways that answer this question. Figure 3.6 depicts the results of several attempts to translate and restate content standards, this time from Illinois.

If Possible, Select and Commit to a Few Standards

For some, accountability means standards written for every concept and skill, for each curriculum, and for every grade. In some cases, this can mean daunting lists of standards. For instance, one state's curriculum standards for communication arts consist of twelve standards, which are further delineated into four or five benchmarks, which are further divided into objectives for early, middle, and high school years. This translates into over one hundred possible standards and benchmarks from which a teacher could choose to teach English and language arts alone. Standards and benchmarks are similarly organized for mathematics, science, social studies, foreign languages, physical education, the arts, and dance. And although there are some fine curriculum ideas spread throughout these documents, there is a good chance that they will be left on the shelf, or on the CD-ROM, unless some attention is devoted to selecting and prioritizing what it really counts for students to learn.

Recent federal legislation, in the form of No Child Left Behind, has spurred the need for very specific standards for early childhood, including preschool, as well as for student performance from kindergarten through grade 8. Starting at age 3, students are expected to progress in their oral language development in preparation for transitioning to reading. Federal programs such as Even Start and Head Start are being refocused to support children's development of early fluency skills, such as understanding the alphabet, letter–sound relationships, and how words are constructed through phonics and phonemic awareness. There is also a new emphasis from the early years through grade 8 on ongoing and standardized assessment, for early intervention and accountability. Mandates, sanctions, and monies are being applied to the states to ensure that these new initiatives are adopted nationwide. Many states, which in the past concerned themselves only with general grade-level standards, are responding to No Child Left Behind by producing yet another series of detailed standards, for preschool and at every grade level, for every subject area. How are we to deal with this proliferation of standards?

Teachers may not always have a choice in the matter, but one answer is to select and commit to a few standards at a time. There are so many worthy standards that can be complex to implement that it makes sense to select a few very important ones and then proceed slowly. One selection strategy consists of evaluating standards in terms of what is important later in life. Figure 3.7 offers examples related to number sense from California middle school mathematics.

FIGURE 3.6 Translating Standards into Plain English

Original Standard	Translation and Restatement
English: Read and understand literature representative of various societies, eras, and ideas.	"This year, we're going to help kids read books, stories and other materials from many different societies, time periods, and points of view. I'm hoping that their experiences will help them better understand different people and ideas throughout history."
Mathematics: Demonstrate and apply a knowledge and sense of numbers, including numeration and operations (addition, subtraction, multiplication, and division), patterns, ratios, and proportions.	"I want my students to really understand numbers and how to work with them. A lot of kids know formulas for addition, subtraction, multiplication, and division, but they don't necessarily know what the operations mean and how they work in real-life situations. I'm going to help them see patterns and really understand how it all works."
Science: Understand the processes of scientific inquiry and technological design to investigate questions, conduct experiments, and solve problems.	"You know, scientists see things a lot differently than you or I. When they start to do an experiment, they set themselves up to make hunches, do experiments, and then make observations, in a lot more detailed way than we do just walking around every day. I want my students to know what it is like to think and act like a scientist."
Social Science: Understand social systems, with an emphasis on the United States.	"We usually take for granted all of the things that happen every day in our society that make things work—the government and politics, the economy, business and industry, and just how people interact day to day. I want students to think about the whole system—we call it the social system—and how it works in our country. At this age, students don't know much about it, but they need to know a lot about it to succeed in life."
Physical Education: Acquire movement skills and understand concepts needed to engage in health-enhancing physical activity.	"A lot of adults struggle with their health their entire lives. In my class, we'll cover how to stay active your whole life. A lot of people struggle to force themselves to exercise, mostly because they don't know how to be active, to keep moving. In my class, we'll learn how to stay active.

Source: Illinois Learning Standards.

Unfortunately, many students arrive in the upper elementary grades, and even middle school and high school, unable to understand or do many of the things specified in Figure 3.7. Consider what life would be like as an adult if you were unable to understand what numbers mean and how they work, as well as

FIGURE 3.7   **Standards Important Later in Life**

Number Sense

Students compare and order positive and negative fractions, decimals, and mixed numbers. Students solve problems involving fractions, ratios, proportions, and percentages:

1.1   Compare and order positive and negative fractions, decimals, and mixed numbers and place them on a number line.

1.2   Interpret and use ratios in different contexts (e.g., batting averages, miles per hour) to show the relative sizes of two quantities, using appropriate notations (*a/b, a* to *b, a:b*).

1.3   Use proportions to solve problems (e.g., determine the value of *N* if $4/7 = N/21$, find the length of a side of a polygon similar to a known polygon). Use cross multiplication as a method for solving such problems, understanding it as the multiplication of both sides of an equation by a multiplicative inverse.

1.4   Calculate given percentages of quantities and solve problems involving discounts at sales, interest earned, and tips.

Students calculate and solve problems involving addition, subtraction, multiplication, and division:

2.1   Solve problems involving addition, subtraction, multiplication, and division of positive fractions and explain why a particular operation was used for a given situation.

2.2   Explain the meaning of multiplication and division of positive fractions and perform the calculations (e.g., $\frac{5}{8} \div \frac{15}{16} = \frac{5}{8} \times \frac{16}{15} = \frac{2}{3}$).

2.3   Solve addition, subtraction, multiplication, and division problems, including those arising in concrete situations that use positive and negative integers and combinations of these operations.

2.4   Determine the least common multiple and the greatest common divisor of whole numbers; use them to solve problems with fractions (e.g., to find a common denominator to add two fractions or to find the reduced form for a fraction).

Source: Mathematics Content Standards for California Public Schools.

the meaning of fractions, decimals, and percents. Not knowing these things would make it very hard to perform such daily activities as making and following a household budget, preparing your tax return, shopping and paying sales taxes and interest charges, paying for things and making change, and even knowing whether one item costs more than another or whether an advertised deal on a car is really a bargain. Beyond such everyday activities, consider what a large role these concepts play in functioning as a good citizen—understanding community priorities and expenditures, evaluating politicians' claims, and even comprehending the meaning of children's school and test performance! There are many other important standards in California and elsewhere, but few carry such a broad impact as this example.

Another strategy for selecting and committing to standards is to seek out standards that cut across all content areas. For instance, there are standards that address the need to interpret maps, charts, and graphs and that consequently apply to science, mathematics, and social studies. Other standards deal with reading and responding to informational texts, such as in English, mathematics, science, and social studies. Rather than treating these standards as discrete and separate, it makes more sense (in terms of time, energy, and transfer) to zero in on these standards, rather than focusing at first on other standards that may be more idiosyncratic and less useful.

In some cases, you may discover standards that have already been developed with this idea in mind. Some standards address thinking, reasoning, and problem solving—areas of performance that permeate all curricular areas. Consider how you might use the standards listed in Figure 3.8.

FIGURE 3.8 Standards that Cut across Content Areas

Gather Information. Research and retrieve information from a wide range of primary and secondary sources in various forms and contexts.

Understand Information. Understand, synthesize, and evaluate information in an accurate, holistic, and comprehensive fashion.

Analyze Issues. Review a question or issue by identifying, analyzing, and evaluating various considerations, arguments, and perspectives.

Draw and Justify Conclusions. Draw and justify conclusions, decisions, and solutions to questions and issues by, among other things, using reason and evidence, specifying goals and objectives, identifying resources and constraints, generating and assessing alternatives, considering intended and unintended consequences, choosing appropriate alternatives, and evaluating results.

Organize and Communicate Information. Organize, present, and communicate information in a variety of media in a logical, effective, and comprehensive manner.

Think and Communicate Critically. Read, listen, think, and speak critically in connection with any subject with clarity, accuracy, precision, relevance, depth, breadth, and logic.

Learn and Consider Issues Collaboratively. Engage in shared inquiry processes, in a collaborative and team-based fashion, with persons of diverse backgrounds and abilities.

Learn Independently. Engage in learning in an active, exploratory, independent, and self-directed fashion.

Create Knowledge. Create knowledge by raising and identifying previously unconsidered or unidentified questions and issues; creating new primary knowledge; and creating new approaches to solving or considering questions and issues.

Act Ethically. Adhere to the highest intellectual and ethical standards in conducting all of the above.

Source: Michigan Learning Expectations.

Finally, in translating, selecting, and committing to a few standards, consider your audience. Parents, school board members, teacher-colleagues, students, and administrators all have different interests in standards. Parents will often be interested in a brief, straightforward description or explanation, with a focus on what your efforts are going to do to help children learn. A school board member might want you to offer a picture of how classrooms are going to change, in relation to standards, especially if she or he is being asked to vote on funding for additional staff development or for instructional and assessment materials connected with standards. Teacher-colleagues desire clear messages about how standards will improve their professional work and students' learning. Students need a personal understanding of standards if they are to live up to expectations that others have of them. And last but not least, administrators are often interested in how standards will change accountability for them, their teachers, and their students.

Of course, it helps tremendously if all of these stakeholders possess similar understandings of the standards you have selected. Better yet, standards can become the center of very productive conversations about change, teaching, and learning when everyone understands and commits to a set of standards.

Prioritize Teaching and Learning

Few teachers have the option to select whatever approach they want. In order to help students perform well on district, state, and national assessments, they must teach to specific state standards. However, given the complexity and shear numbers of standards that are sometimes available, teachers should still try to prioritize the concepts that students need to know.

How can we start to prioritize? And how do we arrive at a combination of activities that will help students make progress? To answer these questions, let's return to our example of the mandates from No Child Left Behind and the development of early reading fluency. Our first job in prioritizing is understanding what the standards mean—in this case, the standards for promoting reading fluency in young children.

Fluent oral reading is reading with smoothness and appropriate expression. It is integral to comprehension in that fluent readers are able to go beyond the specific demands of reading the text to focus on the *meaning* of what they are reading. After the elementary grades, students are expected to read independently. If they have not developed enough reading fluency, the complexity and volume of their required reading overwhelm them (Snow, Burns, et al. 1998).

The teaching of reading fluency has a number of core components (Worthy and Broaddus 2002). These include:

- building a vocabulary of high-frequency words (such as *the, and, these,* and *is*)
- promoting strategies for understanding the relationships between sounds and symbols and for decoding new words
- providing frequent opportunities to practice identifying words through meaningful reading and writing experiences

- helping students transition from word-by-word reading to reading in meaningful phrases
- developing automaticity, or the ability to read quickly while focusing more attention on meaning

There is considerable variation in how children develop reading fluency—variation based on their own patterns of development and on the types and degrees of support they may have available for learning to read (Neuman 1998). For some children, examples of literacy and fluent reading have been all around them from birth: parents reading and writing, children being read to, even formal instruction. For other children, very few literacy experiences are available outside of school. Consequently, some children require different kinds of instruction in fluency than others. Some need the most basic work with learning high-frequency words and decoding words, whereas others need help pulling words together into meaningful phrases.

In this example—developing the standards for reading fluency—what students need and their development of understandings and skill must be assigned the highest priority. To meet students' needs and deal with differences in how children learn, instruction will have to vary. A wide variety of teaching approaches, materials, and strategies must be employed to help children become fluent readers. You will discover that this approach—understanding what the standards mean and thinking about what students already know and how they learn—is invaluable in making choices about what is most important for teaching and learning, whether or not you have choices about which standards you must teach.

SPECIAL PROJECTS

For Beginning Teachers

Using the definitions and examples provided in this chapter, select an existing standard (see the examples throughout this chapter) or write a standard for what you think students should know and be able to do, in literacy or in another content area. How do you think students might differ in their understandings related to the standard? What kinds of teaching and assessment activities would you use to promote this standard?

For Experienced Teachers

Select a set of standards that are closely related to the kind of work you do. For instance, developmental standards may be most appropriate if you are an early childhood educator. Early literacy or mathematics standards may be more appropriate if you are an early elementary educator. If you teach in a middle school or high school, select the appropriate subject area standards. Determine which standards are most important and restate them in plain language. Then describe the kinds of teaching and assessment you might see if the standards you selected were guiding you.

SUGGESTED READING

Reeves, D. (2001). *Making standards work: How to implement standards-based assessments in the class-room, school, and district.* Denver, CO: Center for Performance Assessment.

4 Clarifying and Communicating about Testing

This chapter provides an overview of different kinds of tests, traces some of the history behind them, and then offers some suggestions about how to learn and communicate about the great variety of tests that are used today.

The sheer numbers and kinds of tests available can make it very difficult to understand tests, which ones count the most, which are important for classroom use, and which can best help a teacher, school, or district demonstrate that students are growing and learning in desirable ways. This chapter attempts to shed some light on this issue by providing an overview of the most commonly used tests. Next, it describes ways to communicate effectively about assessment, offering advice based on a careful consideration of tests and their purposes.

National Assessments

A number of tests are given across the United States, largely to determine levels of student achievement. Many school districts use published standardized tests to assess student achievement. These tests have names such as the Metropolitan Achievement Test, the Stanford Achievement Test, and the Iowa Tests of Basic Skills. But even though these tests are administered all over the country, they don't really count as a truly "national" assessment. Schools and districts select different published tests, and it is not always possible to compare results from different tests. The typical purpose for these tests is for schools and districts to gather grade-level snapshots of how students are doing in reading, mathematics, and sometimes writing.

The only current national test is the National Assessment of Educational Progress, also known as the NAEP. Since 1969 the U.S. Department of Education has been responsible for administering the NAEP. The purpose of the NAEP is to assess regularly what American students know and are able to do in various subject areas. Early versions of the NAEP focused on reading, mathematics, and science. This list has since been expanded to include writing, U.S. history, geography, civics, and the arts.

Compared with other tests, national assessments such as the NAEP have very different purposes and implications. The most obvious difference is that student performance on the NAEP has no direct consequence for individual districts, schools, teachers, or students. Individual student scores are not even reported. Instead, results are grouped according to subject matter achievement for the nation and for different regions, instructional and grouping conditions, and targeted populations of students, such as fourth, eighth, and twelfth graders. Results for subgroups (such as males, females, and ethnic groups) are also reported.

NAEP data does play an active role in political, legislative, and public policy arenas. Politicians commonly use NAEP results to make statements about education and reform during political battles. Legislators look at trends in the national data to make decisions about school accountability, where and how to spend money, what programs are working, what programs are not, and what needs to be further developed. Both short- and long-term policy decisions, such as whether to continue early education programs and whether to develop new programs that address school failure, are often based on NAEP data.

Much has been written lately about developing national assessments for high-stakes purposes, such as determining whether children can read at grade 3 and are able to continue on to the next grade (National Reading Panel 2000). However, several factors make this unlikely. First, most states already implement high-stakes assessments in various subject areas. Thus a national battery of tests would duplicate much of the effort that has already been invested at the state level. Second, devising a separate national assessment would involve creating consensus at the national level about what should be taught and assessed. This would be a very complex task, given the differences that already exist in assessment across states and widespread traditions of local control over educational decisions. Finally, developing a new set of national tests would involve considerable time and expense.

A national set of guidelines for testing early literacy has recently emerged. **Reading First** is the name of legislation within No Child Left Behind that specifies the characteristics of early literacy programs and assessment (North Central Regional Educational Laboratory 2003). To receive funding under Reading First, school districts must commit to assessment that

- is built on scientifically based reading research
- represents rigorous standards of proven validity and reliability
- determines the early intervention needs of students at risk for reading failure
- portrays students' progress so that determinations can be made about whether their progress is adequate

Although some states have translated these guidelines into specific tests, most states leave the manner of implementing them up to local schools and districts. As a result, initiatives under No Child Left Behind and Reading First do not lead us any closer to a true national assessment.

State Assessments

State-level assessments have been around for more than half a century. There is some debate about how states got into the business of assessment. Some argue that the trend started after World War II, as businesses became more interested in quality schools that would produce good workers. Others contend that the movement really began during the 1960s, at the height of the Cold War. In the late 1960s, teacher unions were expanding—and teacher strikes were new and frequent. Many state politicians originally viewed state tests as a way of controlling teachers and schools. Ironically, at the same time, teachers' professional associations invested themselves in promoting testing as a way of ensuring quality in schooling. All fifty states have now implemented statewide tests in mathematics, language arts and English, social studies, and science.

Figure 4.1 depicts a typical approach to state test development. Note that test development is a very human, labor-intensive practice. Note too that with most state tests, lots of effort is applied to creating and revising items and to scoring the tests. In most cases, state tests are not standardized. To become standardized, a test needs to be subjected to validation through multiple trials over time, comparisons of known group performance, and detailed statistical analyses. These efforts are costly and time-consuming, which leads many states to do many of the things shown in Figure 4.1 but to stop short of complete standardization (Popham 2003). Because state tests are often not standardized, comparisons of student performance from year to year are usually not recommended, although the media commonly compare student performance as a measure of how schools are doing.

For many years, the consequences for poor student performance on state tests have been relatively benign. School district scores were published in local newspapers, but except for public embarrassment when poor results were reported, there was little pressure for schools or districts to change. With No Child Left Behind, however, there are more serious consequences for schools that do not show consistent growth in student achievement on these tests. Such consequences include

- placement of such schools on probationary status
- mandated tutoring
- increased parent choice for removing students from low-performing schools
- replacement of teachers and administrators
- implementation of new curricula
- extension of the school day or year
- the taking over or closing of schools

Clearly, the use of state-level tests for determining student achievement and school accountability has gained new prominence.

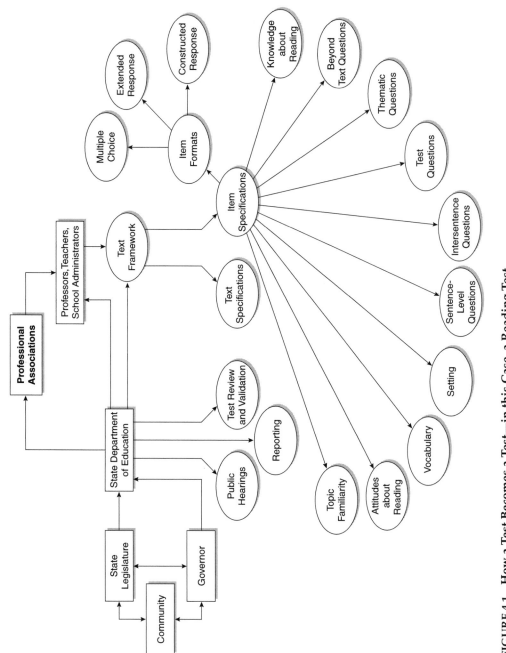

FIGURE 4.1   How a Test Becomes a Test—in this Case, a Reading Test

Local Assessments

The term **local assessments** refers to a whole host of tests that are employed in local schools and classrooms for a variety of purposes. These include school-based tests, early childhood and preschool literacy assessments, teacher-made and published classroom assessments, and even informal reading inventories. These tests and their purposes will be reviewed here.

School-based tests are often used to measure students' progress as they move from grade to grade. Many of these tests accompany published textbooks in reading, mathematics, and other subject areas. Examples include the Houghton Mifflin Integrated Theme tests and the Unit Assessments from Open Court publishers. Some publishers' tests such as Star Reading, are designed more as a supplemental assessment to determine the grade level for which a child is performing. These tests are usually not standardized and instead are created with the publishers' textbook content or skill objectives in mind. Although publishers attempt to connect these tests to state standards, the tests may have very little in common with either state or national standards or assessments. Textbook publishers often claim to align their objectives with standards and assessments, but the result can be a cursory renaming of objectives and tasks that takes little account of what the standards and assessments actually mean. As a result, it is important to be especially vigilant when selecting school-based tests to ensure that they are consistent with other high-stakes assessments.

Early childhood and early literacy assessments take many forms. In some cases, schools and districts craft their own homemade assessments based on their own goals or selection of standards. At other times, schools and districts rely on published and/or standardized assessments. These assessments are used largely to determine students' literacy in areas such as concepts about print, phonemic awareness, alphabetic knowledge, and fluency. (These assessments are covered in Chapter 9.) Recommendations for giving many of these tests involve the use of individual rather than group testing, because group-level testing can be extremely unreliable for younger children. Some have even argued that giving standardized, group-administered tests to children before grade 3 can actually hurt their development and lead to erroneous retention decisions (Stevens and DeBord 2001).

Beyond early literacy and textbook publisher assessments, many different tests are used in classrooms for many different purposes. Informal reading inventories are published tests, often used in classrooms, to assess students' reading achievement. Informal reading inventories are typically individually administered (although with some modifications they can be given in large groups). They include word lists to determine grade-level word recognition, as well as graded passages, through which measures of oral reading fluency and comprehension may be derived. Informal reading inventories often provide grade-level indicators for a child's frustration level, instructional level, and independent reading level.

For example, using the graded passages of an informal inventory, a teacher might discover that a fourth grade student's reading comprehension seriously breaks down at grade 5. That translates into a frustration level of grade 5. At the same time, the student may experience some breakdown in comprehension but still achieve some understandings at grade 4. This translates into an instructional level of grade 4. Finally, the student may demonstrate an independent reading level of grade 3—relatively fluent reading with good comprehension. Teachers use this information in many ways, from determining reading growth over time to making placement decisions for instruction. More detailed information about selecting, administering, and interpreting informal reading inventories, as well as other classroom assessments, appears in Chapter 11.

Teachers also routinely prepare content-specific assessments to determine students' content knowledge as well as their abilities to apply their knowledge in various ways. Because many teacher preparation programs do not focus adequately on assessment, it is still not uncommon for teachers to feel inexperienced in preparing their own classroom-based tests.

In his book *Student-Involved Assessment for Learning*, Richard Stiggins (2005) outlines a set of standards for quality assessment. Quality assessment has the following characteristics:

- **Targets** (goals, objectives, intentions): clearly defined
- **Assessment Methods** (questions, or other kinds of tasks): Appropriate to the targets for the assessment
- **Evaluation** (interpreting performance, scoring, grading): Comprehensible and reasonable
- **Communication:** timely, clear, and consistent

According to Stiggins, teachers who follow this framework in designing classroom tests build a foundation for fair, consistent, and clear assessment.

Communicating about Assessment

Just as there are with standards, there are many choices in assessment and many different reasons for using various tests. This section presents some practices that will help you make good assessment decisions while communicating more effectively about assessment.

Select Tests That Match Your Assessment Purposes

One of my students, an elementary reading teacher, investigated a publisher's reading test that was used in her building. The test had been in use for so many years that no one could remember its purpose. The teacher, feeling that the test was a bit outmoded, asked everyone in her building, and many administrators in her district's central office, why the test was still in use. Finally, she discovered that a reading specialist who had long since retired originally requisitioned the test. She tracked down the reading specialist, and in an interview in the retired teacher's back yard, she asked, "So what was the purpose for that test?" The retired teacher, looking surprised, exclaimed, "They're still using that thing?!"

Unfortunately, as this story demonstrates, a test can take on a life of its own. Some tests are given simply because someone thinks a test of some sort is needed, somewhere, for some reason, but we're not always as careful as we should be in selecting and implementing appropriate tests. And it is easy for "locally grown" classroom tests to be overshadowed by state or even standardized tests. Consequently, it is vitally important that you consider carefully your reasons for testing, striking a balance among the many different types of tests and purposes for testing.

Popham (2003) has introduced the term *instructionally beneficial tests* as one way to prioritize purposes in testing. Instructionally useful tests are those that measure students' achievement of worthwhile curricular goals, such as mastery of a higher-level skill or body of knowledge. Such tests are clearly connected to things that are teachable. Unlike IQ tests or tests of special visualization, instructionally useful tests measure things that can actually be taught, such as specific knowledge or how to do something. Instructionally useful tests are also based on clearly defined standards. In many cases, this means that teachers need to translate existing standards (as described in the last chapter) or develop new standards directly related to what they want students to know and be able to do. Finally, instructionally beneficial tests yield information that helps teachers communicate well.

As you might imagine, many standardized or state-level tests do not fare well under the definition of instructionally beneficial tests (Popham 2003). Many large-scale tests yield only very general information that is most relevant to the assessment of schools or districts. They fail to give teachers much useful information about individual students.

This is not to say that large-scale standardized and state tests should be ignored. What we learn from them is perhaps crucial to accountability at the school, district, and state levels. These purposes do not directly affect teachers and students, but it is necessary to keep these tests in mind, along with the classroom purposes for tests.

What are your instructional purposes for your tests? What are your purposes in testing? And what tests are most beneficial for you in finding out what you, and your students, want to know about how they are doing? Answering these questions for yourself will help you emphasize only those tests that serve a genuine purpose in your classroom and curriculum. Figure 4.2 lists a number of testing purposes and several assessment options for each purpose. Note that a wide range of assessment options can be used to accomplish different kinds of testing purposes. The important thing is that whenever you give a test, you should be able to explain why you are doing it and what you expect to learn from it.

Emphasize Growth *and* Achievement

Large-scale tests—and especially high-stakes tests—usually focus on achievement, what Stiggins calls the **assessment of learning** (Stiggins 2005). As discussed earlier, such tests provide only snapshots of what students have attained. They do not offer a continuous, developing picture of how students come to achieve or fail to achieve. In practice, large-scale state tests often serve as a way to determine

FIGURE 4.2   **Purposes for Tests and Options for Assessment**

Purposes for Tests	Related Assessment Options
■ Finding out what students already know or know how to do	■ Questions at the beginning of a lesson; informal surveys of lesson knowledge and/or tasks; teacher-made and published tests
■ Preventing failure in advance (early intervention)	■ Classroom observations and questions; published tests, informal and standardized tests
■ Keeping track of what students are learning	■ Observations; questions on quizzes or during classroom discussion; published tests
■ Finding out whether students have learned	■ Observations and teacher made questions; published tests; teacher-made, informal, and standardized tests

whom to reward or blame for the level of student achievement they reveal. Tests that assess students' growth offer continuous opportunities to see how students are doing, how they are going about learning, and what sorts of assistance they require to continue growing and learning. Stiggins refers to these assessment purposes and related practices as **assessment for learning** (Stiggins 2005).

Clearly, then, assessing achievement and assessing growth represent two different purposes: achievement per se and learning. Both purposes are important. Achievement-oriented assessments tell administrators, policymakers, teachers, students, and taxpayers how children and schools are doing. Growth-oriented assessments help teachers, students, and even parents find new and better ways for teaching and learning to happen. The potential is great for using both kinds of assessment to improve students' learning *and* to communicate accountability to the public.

For example, student portfolios are an excellent way to document growth. Under the guidance of a teacher, students place samples of their work in a portfolio and learn how to demonstrate how their learning has grown and changed over a period of time. They can also showcase their efforts to do better.

State-level tests, on the other hand, typically lack the day-to-day depiction of growth offered by a portfolio and do not provide nearly as rich a picture of how students are doing. However, parents and the general public have become accustomed to perceiving state tests results as an important indicator of how students are doing. Growth-oriented assessments, such as portfolios, can provide explanations for what happens on large-scale tests. Portfolios can be used to document both how students are progressing toward state goals and assessment targets and what kinds of instruction need to be emphasized to meet students' needs. Growth-oriented assessments offer many opportunities for teachers to help students before they get to the large-scale tests. As a result, it is important to use assessments that focus on growth *and* those that stress on achievement. More information about how to construct and use portfolios appears in Chapter 11.

Communicate about Testing with Respect to Appropriate Purposes

Unfortunately, there is considerable confusion among educators and the public about tests and the purposes for testing. In many cases, parents and the general public expect tests and testing purposes to be identical to those they experienced in school. An accompanying misconception is that all tests are alike and all have the same purpose: to assess achievement. It is often overlooked that tests can help students learn and can even assist parents in helping their children do better. That's why it is imperative that communication about testing be accompanied by information about what tests can do, and what they cannot do, in different situations.

Become accustomed to talking about a test's specific purposes in comparison with other tests, as an integral part of reporting test results. For instance, any discussion of standardized test results should be accompanied by a comparison of standardized tests with your everyday classroom tests. For instance, the following comments compare the snap-shot nature of a standardized test with the information available from an informal test that is given more often.

> We give the standardized test twice a year to see how our students are generally doing with fluency, compared with other students throughout the country. But here are the results of my administration of an informal reading inventory, a test that I can give more frequently to keep track of what students are learning. The standardized test we gave in the fall showed that our students were a bit behind others in the country, but less the results of the informal reading inventory suggest that our students are getting better.

Consider also this comment by a teacher to a parent during a parent–teacher conference:

> I know, the old tests used to emphasize memorizing charts and facts. I took those tests when I was in school too. The new tests are trying to get kids to think more. Here are some examples of how we are working in our class to get up to speed with the new tests. And here are some examples of the ways I am testing the kids in my classroom so that they can be successful on the state tests and even the college entrance tests.

Communicating the appropriate purposes for tests, and how those purposes are different and change from time to time, can be a challenge. But this kind of communication can go a long way toward helping teachers and parents form a partnership for helping students learn.

Consider Your Audience

There are many potential audiences for assessment—parents, administrators, students, colleagues, and even you—but not every audience will be concerned about the same things. Administrators may be more concerned about whether scores on the state tests are going up. Parents often want to know how their child is doing, in relation to your goals and to state standards and assessments. You may be most interested in using assessment as an index of your own effectiveness.

These various interests are all valid, but addressing only one of them can represent an all too narrowly focused perspective. Concentrating on one test, or even on a set of tests, will often not tell the whole story or support good decision making. Be prepared in your own assessment practice to communicate about multiple purposes and perspectives on assessment, so that you can offer the most comprehensive picture possible, even when your audience is unaware of what the complete picture might be—or even of the need to seek it out.

Keep It Simple

Finally, keep messages about assessment as simple and direct as possible. Be sensitive to the potential for confusion about assessment and its many purposes. Applying the ideas contained in this chapter will help you to keep it simple.

SPECIAL PROJECTS

For Beginning Teachers

Visit each of the following websites:

The National Assessment of Educational Progress
http://nces.ed.gov/nationsreportcard/

No Child Left Behind
www.nblb.gov

Metropolitan Achievement Test
www.slosson.com/productCat30137.ctlg

Iowa Test of Basic Skills
www.riverpub.com/products/group/itbs_a/home.html

Scholastic Assessment Test
www.collegeboard.com/

The ACT Test
www.act.org/aap/

What kinds of tests and test practices are portrayed at each website? What kinds of purposes are met by these kinds of tests? What kinds of purposes are not well met by these kinds of tests?

For Experienced Teachers

Investigate the use of tests in your school or district. What tests are used most often? For what purposes are they employed? How appropriate are these tests, given the needs of your students? How appropriate are these tests, given the need to communicate with many different audiences for assessment information?

SUGGESTED READINGS

Calkins, L., Montgomery, K., Santman, D., & Falk, B. (1998). *A teacher's guide to standardized reading tests: Knowledge is Power.* Portsmouth, NH: Heinemann.

Visit the website for the Northwest Regional Educational Laboratories at www.ncrel.org for information about No Child Left Behind and Reading First assessment initiatives.

5 Making Standards Work for You

How to create and implement standards-based lessons and assessments

In working with teachers and doing my own lesson planning, I have often used a five-step process:

- Select
- Adopt
- Adapt
- Invent
- Assess

First, it is important to **select,** or identify, something or some idea or set of concepts that will become the centerpiece for what you want your students to know or be able to do. Second, if the ideas you have selected are sufficiently clear, it will be possible to **adopt** them without much change. In mathematics, for instance, the standards that represent knowledge about fractions quite specifically spell out what students should know (that fractions are parts of a whole, that the line in a fraction really stands for division, and so on). Sometimes, however, concepts have to be **adapted:** They require interpretation so that they can be applied in particular ways for particular students. This often happens with English and social studies standards, but it may occur with science and mathematics standards as well. You may also find yourself in a position where the focus of a lesson or series of lessons requires you to be more innovative: You need to **invent** a perspective or pull together concepts of your own design with regard to something students need to know or be able to do. Finally, when you have an approach to planning that you think is workable, you should stand back and **assess** whether the approach you are taking is the best one. Consider other elements that you may wish to include: instructional materials, perhaps, or teaching activities such as modeling (showing students how to think or perform new skills) and providing practice.

The following sections build on these ideas as this book turns to the task of designing standards-based lessons and assessments.

Selecting Standards for Teaching and Learning

In Chapter 3, we discussed ways to translate standards into plain English and commit to a small number of standards. But let's say you want to zero in on a small number of standards, or even a single standard, to plan a lesson or series of lessons. How do you go about choosing?

There are several criteria you may wish to think about. One consideration concerns the focus at a grade level or within a school building. Because there are so many standards from which to choose, many grade-level teachers, schools, or districts select standards for emphasis within subjects and within grade levels. Although allowing teachers throughout a building to select freely from the many standards that are available may have some appeal, concentrating effort within grades, schools, or districts has many advantages in promoting learning. Select standards for which there seems to be a consensus of agreement and effort. Not all of the standards may be covered within a given period of time, but the students may be more likely actually to learn them.

Another criterion for selecting standards involves what students already know, or how distant the concepts reflected by the standard are in relation to what students know. This is not to say that you should avoid standards about which students know very little. But it may be necessary to start with some standards before launching into others simply because doing so enables students to build on their knowledge. For instance, it might make sense to focus on the skills of scientific observation before getting into standards that require or assume that students can already think like scientists.

Currently, there is a debate about whether young children need to develop reading fluency before they spend a great deal of time learning to comprehend. Some argue that students need to build their listening comprehension before they can gain fluency (Allington 2002). Consult the research and your own experiences, as well as your observations of students, in making these choices.

Designing and Teaching Lessons

Every few years, it seems, a new design for lesson planning seems to pop up. I have observed that these designs always appear to have an odd number of steps— three steps, five, or even seven. The important thing to remember when designing and teaching standards-based lessons is not so much the design steps as the principle that the lesson content must be consistent with the standard(s) you have selected. For purposes of our discussion here, I will choose a three-step lesson design that has a beginning, middle, and end. And, for purposes of our discussion, let's suppose you have selected the following Illinois standard: *Understand the structures and functions of the political systems of Illinois, the United States, and other nations.* And let's imagine that your interest in this standard is at the middle school level, where the focus is on identifying what the government does at the local, state, and national levels.

> **The lesson content needs to be consistent with the standard(s).**

Beginnings.   Beginnings of lessons usually focus on the following activities: assessing and activating students' prior knowledge, motivating students, and introducing the knowledge and skills that students will learn. In the case of our selected standard, an important concept is the whole idea of government. A key assessment question therefore, is "How much do students know about the structure and operations of government at local, state, and national levels?" Answering this question requires making some hunches about what students already know. For instance, many adolescents have some sense of government from listening to their parents. A small number may be on Student Council, the operation of which is probably a far cry from the functioning of government in the public arena. Thus an important task at the beginning is getting students to know more and to become motivated to know more about government.

> **Beginnings of lessons assess and activate prior knowledge, motivate students, and introduce the standard(s).**

There are, of course, many ways to introduce this topic. One way is to ask students how decisions are made within their own families. (As in a dictatorship? Democratically? What types of decisions get made?) This discussion of family governance could lead to an exploration of how decisions are made in our society and to the idea of local, state, and national governments.

The Middle.   Middles of lessons usually build knowledge about the selected standard(s). This is often referred to the meat of the lesson. Again, activities chosen here need to be consistent with the selected standard(s).

> **Middles of lessons develop content knowledge and must be consistent with the standard(s).**

Back to our hypothetical social studies lesson. Once students have an initial understanding of governments, a teacher might want to stress types and functions. The exercise shown in Figure 5.1 might prove useful. Readings from a textbook, the Internet, or government documents could be selected to help students fill in this figure. Additionally, guest speakers could be brought in from different levels of government to explain what they do.

FIGURE 5.1 Developing Content for a Social Studies Lesson

Directions: By placing an X in the appropriate blanks, indicate which kind(s) of government(s) is (or are) responsible for the following jobs. In the space below, explain your answers.

Jobs

Governments	Snow Plowing	Collecting Taxes	Licensing Drivers	Defending our Country
Local government				
State government				
National government				

_____

_____

_____

_____

Endings.   As experienced teachers know, there are never any real endings to lessons. Ideally, knowledge gained from one lesson becomes the foundation for later knowledge and applications—or, in our case, for the teaching and learning of additional standards. In our hypothetical lesson, the student activities that we might select include conducting interviews with parents and others about government; writing letters to government officials, asking questions about their jobs; and reading more about how government functions in different situations, from shaping public decision making to fighting crime and improving schools. These activities also provide opportunities to assess how well students understand what they have learned and to determine whether you will need to reteach some of the standard-related concepts.

> **Lessons never really end; they provide a foundation for building more understandings about standards.**

Later lessons might take up the students' roles as citizens in society and government, reflected in another Illinois standard: awareness of how citizens and groups shape government policy and decision making. In other words, earlier lessons might focus on the parts and functions of the government, and later lessons might personalize students' roles and responsibilities within various levels of government.

Revising and Redesigning Published Materials

Although many publishers attempt to market classroom materials with standards in mind, it is with varying degrees of success. Many publishers try to pack in as many instructional activities as possible as part of their marketing. However, not all of these activities are related specifically to a set of standards. This can pose problems for developing students' understandings of standards.

This is where we need to return to the five-step model introduced at the beginning of this chapter: select, adopt, adapt, invent, and assess. To revise and redesign published materials, start again as we did before: *Select* a standard. Next, review the published materials. Which concepts and activities will help students understand the targeted standard? *Adopt* the activities that are most relevant. Mark or underline the activities that will work the best. Some activities may require a bit of tweaking, so *adapt* those activities to the purposes and concepts related to the standard. In some cases, after going through this process, you may discover that you need to *invent* activities beyond the published materials so that students will really understand the standard. Finally, *assess* to reveal any activities that don't work well in developing the standard.

The example shown in Figure 5.2, taken from an elementary reading text, illustrates how this process works. The title of this text is *Trapped in Tar: Fossils from the Ice Age,* and the standard chosen is about problem solving—in this case, uncovering the mystery behind the extinction of dinosaurs and the discovery of fossils in the La Brea tar pits (Cooper and Pikulski 1999).

Developing Teaching and Learning Strategies

Once you have identified standards and prepared lesson(s) that follow from the standards, there are other factors to consider. The next several sections discuss ways to build literacy while promoting standards-based understandings.

Creating Opportunities for Reading

Many standards lend themselves to having students do outside "research," either through books and magazines or through movies and the Internet. For the standard shown in Figure 5.3, the resources shown in Figure 5.4 were gathered readily, through a quick Internet search (www.google.com) using the search term "books for kids" + ecosystem.

It is also important to be sensitive to any special challenges presented by the standard(s) with which you are working. One challenge concerns **comprehension:**

FIGURE 5.2   **Revising Curriculum Materials with Standards in Mind**

English Standard Selected (from Illinois State Goals for Learning)	Text Topics and Activities	Lesson-Planning Decisions
Recognize and investigate problems; formulate and propose solutions.	Prior knowledge activity: Quick-write about fossils	**Adopt**—This is a good activity for assessing and building prior knowledge
	Vocabulary activity: asking questions about key vocabulary words	**Adapt**—This may not be enough to build the knowledge. Select some pictures from the student text to illustrate the words.
	Spelling pretest, challenge words	**Discard**—The spelling words do not contribute to the standard or to understanding of the material
	Comprehension skills: summarizing and evaluating	**Adapt**—Need to stress problem solving. Key question: How did the fossils get in the tar pits?
	Guided reading: asking questions	**Invent**—The text questions are not helpful in understanding the problem(s) written about in the text. Need to write new questions that focus on the basic problems and solutions that appear in the text and are emphasized in the standard.
	Writing: developing explanations	**Adapt**—The explanation activity is not very motivating. Change it to a news report for television. Create, with students, a template that involves the problem solution concepts from the standard.
	Word skills and strategies	**Discard**—Students already know how to do these skills and do not need additional work.
	Grammar exercise	**Discard**—The grammar exercise does not enhance understanding of the standard. Grammar is dealt with more effectively in the curriculum in other ways.

FIGURE 5.3   Florida Standard in Science

The student understands the consequences of using limited natural resources.

1. Knows that layers of energy-rich organic materials have been gradually turned into great coal beds and oil pools (fossil fuels) by the pressure of the overlying earth and that humans burn fossil fuels to release the stored energy as heat and carbon dioxide.
2. Knows that changes in a component of an ecosystem will have unpredictable effects on the entire system but that the components of the system tend to react in a way that will restore the ecosystem to its original condition.
3. Understands how genetic variation of offspring contributes to population control in an environment and that natural selection ensures that those who are best adapted to their surroundings survive to reproduce.
4. Knows that the world ecosystems are shaped by physical factors that limit their productivity.
5. Understands that the amount of life any environment can support is limited and that human activities can change the flow of energy and reduce the fertility of the Earth.
6. Knows the ways in which humans today are placing their environmental support systems at risk (e.g., rapid human population growth, environmental degradation, and resource depletion).

Source: Florida Sunshine State Standards for Science, grades 9–12.

FIGURE 5.4   Resources Gathered in Support of a Standard for the Study of Humans in the Ecosystem

Craighead-George, J. (1972). *Julie of the wolves.* New York: Harper & Row, 1972. This is a story about a girl who learns to survive in the arctic with the help of a wolf pack.

Soylent Green, a movie about overpopulation and dwindling food resources.

Crew, L. (1990). *Fire on the wind.* New York: Laurel Leaf Books. This book is about a teenage girl who survives the Tillamook logging fires of 1933.

www.muskox.com/bill/books.shtml This official website for the Institute for Field Education specializes in arctic ecology.

how difficult the readings are to understand and what difficulties are posed by what you (and the standard) ask students to do in order to understand. Reading comprehension is defined as "an active process that requires an intentional and thoughtful interaction between the reader and the text." (National Reading Panel 2000). Figure 5.5 presents some strategies you might find useful in helping

FIGURE 5.5 Comprehension Strategies

Vocabulary instruction: Teaching and learning vocabulary words ahead of time. Words selected should be important to understanding in the context of a subject or reading material in order to increase Comprehension.

Comprehension monitoring: Students learn to be aware of their understanding of the text and to use specific strategies when needed. Comprehension monitoring is "thinking about thinking." Ask students questions like: "What do you know now?" "What do you not understand at this point?" Share some strategies that you use when you get "stuck" while reading.

Cooperative learning: Students work together to learn comprehension strategies. This leads to an increase in the learning of the strategies, promotes intellectual discussion, and increases reading comprehension. Select times when the use of cooperative learning will be most productive, in situations involving controversy and where students have some background knowledge.

Graphic organizers: Students write or draw meanings and relationships of underlying ideas. Drawing pictures and diagrams improves a reader's memory for the content that has been read. Demonstrate how to map out ideas so that students can learn to do this on their own.

Story structure: Students ask and answer who, what, when, where, why, how. Students can also map time lines, characters, and story events.

Question answering: Teachers pose questions and guide students to correct answers, enabling them to learn more from the text. Extend this work by having students learn to ask and answer their own questions, based on your modeling.

Question generating: Students ask themselves what, where, when, why, what will happen, how, and who questions.

Summarization: Students identify and write the main ideas of a story, or the key ideas in informational materials.

Source: International Reading Association's (2003) Summary of the (U.S.) National Reading Panel Report "Teaching Children to Read."

students comprehend better, especially when standards present some real reading challenges.

Creating Opportunities for Thinking

A great many standards lend themselves to instructional experiences where you can help students learn to think for themselves. Consider a mathematics example from the Texas Essential Knowledge and Skills for Science (Figure 5.6).

Like many standards, this standard presents a general situation that needs to be provided a specific context. In this case, consider the various kinds of contexts that would get students to think. A good starting point would be their own

FIGURE 5.6   **Helping Students Think for Themselves**

The student is expected to:

(A) plan and implement investigative procedures including asking questions, formulating testable hypotheses, and selecting and using equipment and technology;

(B) collect data by observing and measuring;

(C) organize, analyze, evaluate, make inferences, and predict trends from direct and indirect evidence;

(D) communicate valid conclusions; and

(E) construct graphs, tables, maps, and charts using tools including computers to organize, examine, and evaluate data.

Source: Texas Essential Knowledge and Skills for Science.

conceptions and misconceptions about scientific exploration. For instance, thought-provoking topics for this standard could include

- Folkloric cures versus scientific cures for the common cold: What really works?
- Is the earth really getting warmer? How do we know?

Ideally, students should be involved in the brainstorming for these issues and activities. It is intriguing to discover that even very young children can become involved in collecting data and in representing information accurately through charts and graphs, if the topic is sufficiently accessible. (For instance, they can measure outside temperatures over time, and they can represent the results of a poll in an elementary school about cures for colds.)

Creating Opportunities for Writing

Because many of the standards naturally focus on comprehension and thinking skills, there may be many built-in opportunities for student writing. Take care in finding places where writing will be natural and appropriate. Different standards imply different kinds of writing. Consider, for example, the types of writing implied by the Virginia standard shown in Figure 5.7.

A common mistake is to attach complicated writing activities to already complicated standards. For instance, many times in mathematics and science, the best kinds of writing ask students simply to summarize what they know at various points in a lesson or unit or what they have learned overall. Do not overlook, however, opportunities for writing that take students from subject matter standard to real-world writing. Consider this standard in mathematics, science, and technology from New York:

> ## Mathematics, Science, and Technology
>
> **Standard 1: Analysis, Inquiry, and Design**
> Students will use mathematical analysis, scientific inquiry, and engineering design, as appropriate, to pose questions, seek answers, and develop solutions.
>
> *Source:* New York State Learning Standards.

Now consider a common topic in mathematics: measurement. Pose the following problem: "What would happen if the distance between the planets were mismeasured, because the scientists used the English system when they meant to use the metric system?" This problem actually arose in 1999, when NASA miscalculated speed, velocity, and distance in sending out probes to Mars. This type of problem could easily engage students in various kinds of mathematical research, descriptions, and explanations, all involving writing. To design assignments like this, start with a standard, think about a real-life situation or problem, and then consider how writing could be used to help students gain both a greater appreciation of the standard and better proficiency in writing.

FIGURE 5.7   Types of Writing Implied by a Standard

Standard

Conflict: The World at War: 1939 to 1945	Type(s) of Writing
The student will demonstrate knowledge of World War II by:	
a) identifying the causes and events that led to American involvement in the war, including military assistance to Britain and the Japanese attack on Pearl Harbor;	descriptive writing, lists of details
b) describing the major battles and turning points of the war in North Africa, Europe, and the Pacific, including Midway, Stalingrad, the Normandy landing (D-Day), and Truman's decision to use the atomic bomb to force the surrender of Japan;	descriptive writing, persuasive writing
c) describing the role of all-minority military units, including the Tuskegee Airmen and Nisei regiments;	descriptive writing
d) describing the Geneva Convention and the treatment of prisoners of war during World War II; and	research, descriptive writing
e) analyzing the Holocaust (Hitler's "final solution"), its impact on Jews and other groups, and postwar trials of war criminals.	research, persuasive writing

Source: Virginia Standards of Learning.

Creating Opportunities for Communicating

Many standards are written to focus explicitly on standards for oral language, such as the Wisconsin standards shown in Figure 5.8.

Other standards have embedded within them implicit messages that oral language is essential. Consider Figure 5.9, physical education standards from California for fourth graders. It would be nearly impossible to approach these standards without relying on oral language.

FIGURE 5.8   Wisconsin Standard for Oral Language

Orally communicate information, opinions, and ideas effectively to different audiences for a variety of purposes.

- Identify and discuss criteria for effective oral presentations, including such factors as eye contact, projection, tone, volume, rate, and articulation
- Read aloud effectively from previously read material
- Speaking from notes or a brief outline, communicate precise information and accurate instructions in clearly organized and sequenced detail
- Present autobiographical or fictional stories that recount events effectively to large and small audiences
- Participate in group readings, such as choral, echo, and shadow reading
- Perform dramatic readings and presentations
- Distinguish between fact and opinion and provide evidence to support opinions

Listen to and comprehend oral communications.

- Follow basic directions
- Identify and summarize key points of a story or discussion
- Retell stories and reports of events in proper sequence
- Follow sequence in plot and character development, predict outcomes, and draw conclusions
- Recall the content of stories after hearing them, relate the content to prior knowledge, and answer various types of factual and interpretive questions about the stories
- Distinguish fact from fantasy and fact from opinion
- Understand increasingly complex sentence structures
- Understand a variety of word structures and forms, such as affixes, roots, homonyms, antonyms, synonyms, and word analogies

Participate effectively in discussion.

- Volunteer relevant information, ask relevant questions, and answer questions directly
- Use appropriate eye contact and other nonverbal cues
- Use appropriate strategies to keep a discussion going
- Reflect on the ideas and opinions of others and respond thoughtfully
- Ask for clarification and explanation of unfamiliar words and ideas
- Summarize information conveyed through discussion

Source: Wisconsin Model Academic Standards for Language Arts, Grade 4.

FIGURE 5.9   Oral Language in Physical Education

Personal Development

Standard 5. The student will demonstrate responsible personal behavior while participating in movement activities.
Students in grade four who meet this standard will be able to:

- Assess their own performance problems without blaming others.
- Accept decisions regarding a rule infraction without displaying a negative reaction.
- Act in a safe manner during physical activity.
- Work independently and on task for small-group activities.

The following is an assignment that might be used to meet the standard:

- Students are divided into small groups to work on pitching, batting, and catching a Wiffle ball. Students will set up equipment and practice each skill in a cooperative manner. After completion of the activity, students will assess their own performance in (1) cooperating in the group; (2) being helpful; and (3) ensuring equal practice time for all.

Social Development

Standard 6. The student will demonstrate responsible social behavior while participating in movement activities. The student will understand the importance of respect for all others.
Students in grade four who meet this standard will be able to:

- Demonstrate the ability to lead or follow while working cooperatively with a partner or small group.
- Recognize the fundamental strategies in simple games.
- Recognize the attributes that individual differences can bring to group activities.

The following is a task that might be used to meet the standard:

- Students in small groups decide, from a set of specific game skills, which skills their groups will practice. Students will ensure that each member of the group gets the appropriate amount of practice on the skill to ensure group success. Members of each group will work to help one another improve, and the group will stay focused on the task.

Source: California Learning Standards, Physical Education Standards, Grade Four.

The important thing to remember is that students do not automatically have the skills necessary to accomplish activities implied by these standards. In many cases, you may wish to create specific lessons that promote oral language development, especially those that place students in real-life situations, such as giving and following oral directions, providing an explanation, and making an oral argument.

During these kinds of lessons and at other times when stressing oral language, it is important to model the behaviors students are supposed to learn. A prime example of this concerns learning to discuss or make decisions in groups. Just throwing students into a group and saying "Discuss!" is not nearly so effective as describing group roles and responsibilities, explaining what students need to do to work with one another, and engaging in some role playing to demonstrate healthy group discussion and what to do when discussion breaks down. Teaching students how to engage in roles necessary for group discussion is also important. Giving all students practice in taking group roles, such as facilitator, fact finder, and summarizer can often break through students' social biases, helping students who are often excluded to become part of the larger group.

Do not assume that students know how to handle themselves with communication in other classroom situations or during individual communication. Many teachers begin the school year by introducing and modeling norms for student behavior during whole-class discussions and seatwork. With each standard, ask the following questions:

- What will students need to be able to do to accomplish the specific oral language activities?
- What do students already know how to do? What do they need to learn?

Answers to these questions should lead naturally to the design of explicit teaching and modeling activities to help students use oral language in desired ways.

Group Discussion Roles

Reporter/Recorder	*Opinion seeker*	*Summarizer*
Facilitator	*Fact finder*	*Clarifier*

SPECIAL PROJECTS

For Beginning Teachers

Select a standard from the standards found in this book, or from your state standards. Look on the Internet for your state Department of Education to locate your state's standards. Now choose an audience of students: early elementary, upper elementary, middle school, or high school. Describe a simple lesson—with a beginning, a middle, and an end—to teach the standard. Tell how you will know students understand the standard you have selected.

For Experienced Teachers

Select a standard within your subject area and grade level. List the topics and activities within a set of published materials that you have available. Next to this list, make another column and decide whether you need to adopt, adapt, invent, or discard activities on your list. Describe ways in which you will need to modify activities that you need to adapt. List activities that you will need to create, so that you can do a better job of emphasizing the standard you have selected.

SUGGESTED READINGS

Atwell, N. (1998). *In the middle: New understanding about writing, reading, and learning.* Portsmouth, NH: Heinemann.

Calkins, L. (1994). *The art of teaching writing.* Portsmouth, NH: Heinemann.

Cohen, E., & Goodlad, J. (1994). *Designing group work.* New York: Teachers College Press.

Hurt, J. (2003). *Taming the standards: A commonsense approach to higher student achievement, K–12.* Portsmouth, NH: Heinemann.

Marzano, R., Pollack, J., & Pickering, D. (2001). *Classroom instruction that works: Research-based strategies for increasing student achievement.* Alexandria, VA: Association for Supervision and Curriculum Development.

Shulman, J., Lotan, R., Whitcomb, J., & Darling-Hammond, L. (1998). *Groupwork in diverse classrooms: A casebook for educators.* New York: Teachers College Press.

CHAPTER

6

When "Teaching to the Test" Is Just Good Curriculum

The distinction between teaching to the test and integrating test-taking skills into the curriculum—and how to do the latter

What Is Teaching to the Test and Why Do We Fear It?

To many, **teaching to the test** means using practice test items, released items, and (in some cases) the actual test items to get students ready for tests. However, teaching to the test can also mean teaching a body of knowledge or skills represented by a test.

In this second case, the teacher may recognize that the knowledge and skills in the test reflect valued curricula, something students need to know and be able to do. Popham (2001) distinguishes between these two definitions for teaching to the test by referring to **item teaching**—using rote or cloned items to teach directly to a test—and **curriculum teaching**—teaching that is directed at the valued content of the curriculum, usually assessed by some form of testing.

Item-teaching makes many of us uncomfortable, because we feel that teaching only what is on the test diminishes students' experiences with more important curricula. To be sure, a curriculum made up only of how to answer multiple-choice questions or how to craft essays would be boring and not very useful. More important, spending too much time on these activities takes away from more critical understandings and skills that students need. On the other hand, a modest amount of rehearsal in advance of a high-stakes test is important if students are to connect what they have learned in the curriculum with the question and answer formats of the test. Striking an appropriate balance between curriculum teaching and building an awareness of the structure of test items is the key.

Over many years, I have observed teachers and administrators heroically struggling with the onslaught of standards and tests, in every content area, at every grade level. The reasons are fairly simple: tremendous pressure for schools to do better and passion to help students do the best they can. Faced with the pressures of high-stakes assessment, many educators feel that they have no choice but to emphasize individual test-taking skills. But an analysis of the test-taking skills within tests across content areas illustrates just how complex a proposition this can be.

Item-Based Test-Taking Skills

Most state tests consist of three types of test items: multiple-choice, constructed response and extended-response items. Each of these types requires different kinds of skill in responding (Stiggins 2005). Some teachers rehearse students in responding to these items as preparation for state tests. The demands of each of these types of items are not always obvious.

Multiple-choice items are familiar to most people as consisting of a question or statement, sometimes referred to as the *stem,* accompanied by four choices or selections, sometimes referred to as the *foils.* Only one foil represents the correct answer. To deal with multiple-choice items, students need not only the knowledge reflected in the item but also the skill of discriminating one possible answer from another. This skill can be very complex, as illustrated by the multiple-choice item in Figure 6.1, which asks students to select one theme over others in reference to two separate texts.

Constructed-response items ask students to supply information, which may range in length from short answers (sometimes only a word or two) all the way up to a sentence or even a paragraph, in response to a question. To answer constructed-response questions, the student not only must know the content to supply, but also must understand exactly what sort of response the question requires. For example, the constructed-response item in Figure 6.2 calls for a position statement, or a point of view, and a reason for taking that position.

Extended-response items ask students to write longer responses, such as descriptive or persuasive essays. Some tests, especially writing tests, require a response based on personal experiences. Many tests require some form of response to selected readings and/or the recall of subject matter knowledge. Like constructed-response items, extended-response items call for an understanding of what the question is asking, as well as for specific kinds of content knowledge and/or personal experience. Students may have difficulty understanding the kind of response required (story, description, persuasion) and how to craft the appropriate response (see Figure 6.3).

FIGURE 6.1   A Multiple-Choice Item Based on Themes

"The Open Window" and "The Importance of Fiction" are SIMILAR because they show that:

1. effective communication leads to misunderstanding.
2. effective communication can change people's lives.
3. creativity is not essential to being understood.
4. human experiences are not important.

FIGURE 6.2 **A Constructed-Response Item**

On the lines provided for this item in the answer booklet, state your position on whether or not affirmative action has been effective in establishing justice. Give one reason that explains your position.

Your Position: _____

_____

_____

Your Reason:_____

_____

_____

FIGURE 6.3 **An Extended-Response Item**

Think about a talent or skill you have or would like to have. It may be telling stories, making people laugh, playing a game, or being a good listener. **Write about a talent or skill.** You might, for example, do *one* of the following:

Write about a time when you decided you wanted to be good at something.
OR
Describe how someone might get better at a talent or skill.
OR
Write about a time when someone first discovered a talent or skill.
OR
Describe a talent or skill you would like to have.
OR
Write about the topic in your own way.

You may use examples from real life, from what you read or watch, or from your imagination.

Your writing will be read by interested adults.

One could envision a curriculum focused entirely on these various item-specific skills. However, there are a number of problems and ethical issues involved in pursuing such an approach. Consider what would happen to the content—reading quality literature; relating mathematics, science, and social studies to everyday living; making curriculum standards come alive—if teachers focused only on the skills involved in answering multiple-choice, constructed-response, and extended-response questions. To be sure, students would very quickly become bored and would not be well served if all they ever did was rehearse for tests by studying item types. Additionally, studying item types alone fails to take into account the skills that are specific to state tests.

Test-Specific Skills

In grappling with the demands of state tests, many educators have constructed charts based on taking the tests and thinking out loud about the mental steps required to be successful on the tests. Consequently, their intention is to devise curricula that help their student be more successful on the tests. The charts shown in Figures 6.4 through 6.8 were constructed through research involving think-alouds while students were responding to items on state tests in reading/language arts, writing, mathematics, science, and social studies (Conley 2001).

Each chart represents the cognitive tasks or steps that one might use to answer items on each of the tests.

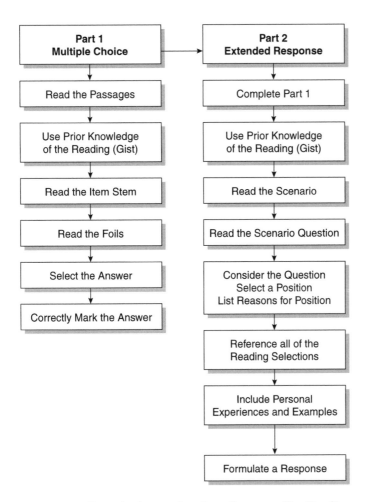

FIGURE 6.4   Steps in Answering Questions on a Reading/Language Arts Test with Response to Reading

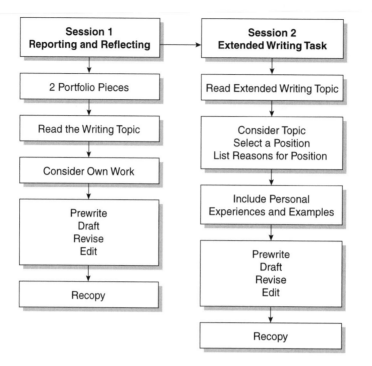

FIGURE 6.5   Steps in Answering Questions on a State Writing Test

My experience has been that these activities are often isolated with subject areas and grade levels. Envision an elementary school with six grade levels with small groups of teachers within subject areas, grade levels, or both, all constructing charts like this and spending energy on getting students to understand and do all of these skills! Now consider the experience of their students, moving from class to class, being exposed to a new set of discrete skills implied by all of the assessments, and then having to transfer these understandings to the actual test-taking situation. It is no wonder that, even with responsible effort targeted at the curriculum reflected in the tests, we fear the results of these efforts. But it does not have to be this complicated, nor does the curriculum need to be reduced to a mere exercise in preparation for tests. In the following section, we will take up and define the essential test-taking skills that everyone can adopt as part of a valued curriculum.

The Essential Test-Taking Skills

Looking across the tests depicted earlier, we note that a small number of skills begin to emerge. These essential test-taking skills reach across all subject areas and are ap-

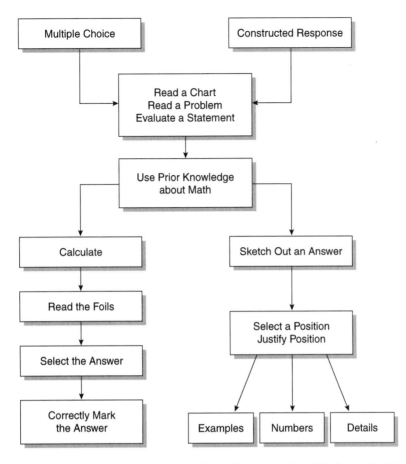

FIGURE 6.6   Steps in Answering Questions on a State Mathematics Test

plicable from the earliest grades on into high school. These skills are described in the following sections, which also include an explanation for each and examples.

Understanding and Distinguishing between Big and Small Ideas

Many tests draw on students' abilities to understand and tell the difference between big and small ideas. The most obvious place where this occurs is in short and more extended writing prompts on tests in all content areas. For instance, examine the test questions from Washington State that appear in Figure 6.9. The big ideas are represented by the questions themselves. Students are required to supply the big ideas (a position or stand) and the details (support for the position or stand) in order to be successful on the assessment.

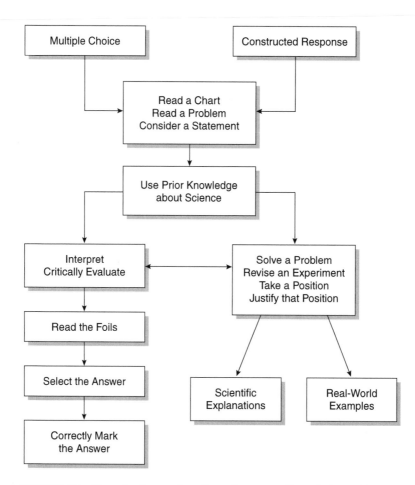

FIGURE 6.7   Steps in Answering Questions on a State Science Test

Not surprisingly, students do not exhibit these skills automatically. Less skilled writers, for example, often get lost in the details and never mention a position, or they restate what they think or feel over and over again, without ever backing it up. To be successful, students need to do both: They must take a position *and* thoughtfully back it up with reasons or evidence.

Big and small ideas are also an important part of responding to multiple-choice items. Consider Figure 6.10, which gives sample item specifications, again from Washington State. Item specifications are a recipe for how to write items on a test. In this case, the recipe is for how to write an item to determine an author's message, a big idea. In these types of items, details are often thrown in as incorrect answers. As you might expect, students who do not understand the difference between big and small ideas do not do very well on these kinds of multiple-choice questions. Consider what happens in your daily teaching when students fail to understand the differences between big and small ideas. They fail to understand

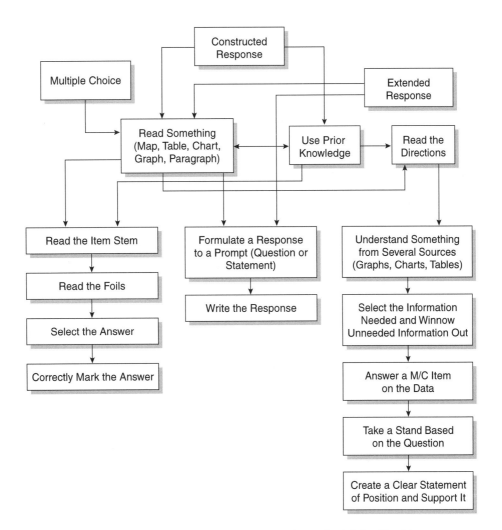

FIGURE 6.8   Steps in Answering Questions on a State Social Studies Test

big thematic connections that reflect the core ideas and standards that underlie the curriculum. When they *do* grasp the big ideas, however, they can build on these understandings and see interconnections among the important details.

Analyzing Questions

Are your students proficient at analyzing an assignment and performing exactly in ways that you expect, either creatively or in synthesizing what they have learned? It is not uncommon for very young children and struggling learners to experience difficulty with this skill. Lack of ability in this area surfaces in all sorts of ways when students perform on high-stakes tests.

FIGURE 6.9   **Assessments That Work with Big and Small Ideas**

Writing, Grade 7

Many students in your school feel they should have a 10-minute break in the morning and in the afternoon. Decide if you agree or disagree with this proposal. Write a multiple-paragraph letter to your principal in which you try to persuade him or her to support your position.

Mathematics, Grade 7

Two students measured the width of a classroom to the nearest unit. The first student used a toothpick as a unit, and the second used a broomstick as a unit. Which one had a measurement that was more precise? Clearly explain your answer using words, pictures, and/or numbers.

Source: Adapted from Washington Assessment of Student Learning.

FIGURE 6.10   **Big and Small Ideas in Multiple-Choice Items**

Item Type: Author's Message

Example of stem:

What do you think the author is telling readers in this story?

Example of response choices:

a. The correct response is the best statement of the message of the story.
b. One incorrect response is not the best statement of the message because it contains an idea not included in the passage.
c. One incorrect response is not the best statement of the message because it contains an unimportant idea that is stated in the passage.

Example of stem:

The message of this poem has to do with sharing. Which of the following ideas from the poem helps get this message across?

Example of response choices:

a. The correct response is a detail that supports the message.
b. One incorrect response is a detail in the poem that does not support the message.
c. One incorrect response is a detail that appears to support the message but is not actually included in the selection.

Source: Washington Assessment of Student Learning.

This problem is exacerbated by complicated, multipart test questions, such as those that appear in Figure 6.11. Although they are intended to give students lots of choices and guidelines, these types of questions can also represent too complex a maze of choices and pathways down which many students can get lost. Note also in this example how many of these test questions rely on students' knowledge of vocabulary to understand what they are to produce. In the cases shown here, if students do not understand the terms *public policy issue, position, support, core democratic value, opposite point of view* and *flaws in his or her argument*, they will have considerable difficulty in answering these questions.

Going back to our original question, how many times have you handed out an assignment only to see the hands raised and/or the blank stares indicating that students do not understand what you are asking them to do? When one considers that life is full of new and sometimes incomprehensible tasks (such as going to the license bureau, passing tests in college or trade school, and signing for a mortgage), it is clear that the skill of analyzing questions is an essential part of any curriculum.

Getting Organized

Once a student figures out what to do to in response to a testing task or classroom assignment, it is important for her or him to get organized before diving

---

FIGURE 6.11   Multipart Questions

Taking a Stand (Social Studies)

You will now take a stand on the following public policy issue: Should high schools establish student courts to deal with discipline? You may either support or oppose a student court. Write a letter to the president of the school board. Use the following criteria to provide reasons that support your position.

You will be graded on the following criteria. Your letter must include:

- a clear and supporting statement of your position;
- supporting information using a core democratic value of American constitutional democracy;
- supporting knowledge from history, geography, civics (other than the core democratic values), or economics (it is not enough to state only your opinion);
- supporting information from the Data Section of this question; and
- a credible argument someone from the opposite point of view could use and an explanation that reveals the flaw in his/her argument

Remember to:

Use complete sentences
Explain your reasons in detail
Explain how the core democratic value you use connects to your position
Write or print neatly on the lines provided in your answer book

---

Source: Michigan Educational Assessment Program.

into a response. Many students who do not do well on high-stakes tests have difficulty because they are unable to organize their responses. This can take a variety of forms, including failure to

- mention the question they are answering
- present an argument or point of view, providing details or lists of facts instead
- organize an answer in terms of cause and effect, comparison/contrast, or time order
- summarize their point of view; or
- provide enough information or details to receive full credit

Consider this relatively simple-looking question:

> **Explain two ways air pollution is caused by changes in matter. For each way, explain what substance is being changed and what it is being changed into.**
> *Source:* Michigan High School Test in Science.

There are a number of ways in which answers could go wrong with this question. Students could name the ways but not discuss the substances or the changes. They could mention that air pollution is bad and never talk about matter or how changes in it cause pollution. They could launch into solutions for pollution and never talk about the changes in matter. An organized response, however, would start by referring to the question (*There are two ways air pollution is caused by changes in matter*). It would continue by naming the ways and then explain how matter is involved and what changes actually take place, from one state to another. All of that is implied by the question, but many students do not even know how to get started.

Again, a useful lifelong skill, applicable across the curriculum, involves getting organized to respond to a task that one has been asked to perform—a question, a directive, a challenge. Helping students get organized is a useful goal for success both in and out of school.

Thinking about What You Already Know

Many high-stakes tests require students to use their content knowledge, especially in mathematics, science, and social studies. Trying to predict what concepts are going to be favored from subject to subject, grade to grade, and year to year often drives teachers and administrators crazy. Even more maddening is ensuring not only that students internalize what they need to know but also that they are able to transfer their knowledge to the tests.

A major barrier to this happening concerns students' tendency to rush through questions without ever thinking about what they already know and how it is related to what they need to do to answer the questions. Connecting this problem to the classroom, we often hope that students build knowledge throughout the school year, but unless we remind students of what they already know, they will not make the necessary connections. That is why this skill is included in our list of essential test-taking skills.

Taking a Stand on Content

As we have observed already, many high-stakes tests require students to take a stand, adopt a point of view, assume a perspective. Although we most often associate this skill with English (proving something about a story or defending a point of view about an issue) or social studies (taking a perspective on history, politics, or economics), the notion of taking a stand is also strongly represented in science and mathematics. Take, for example, the items show in Figure 6.12. Answering the science question requires an understanding and application of scientific concepts such as nutrition and metabolism. Students who answer this question without thinking about what they know scientifically could easily rely instead on general knowledge or misconceptions. Similarly, the mathematics question calls for a specific application of knowledge about percents and algebra. Students who fail to consider what they know will be unable to find an "entry point" into the question.

Just like the previously described skills, thinking about what you know is important throughout the curriculum and later in life. How many times have you been in a situation that called for some special knowledge that you forgot or were too busy to think about? Slowing down and considering what you know is an important life skill that many children and adolescents must learn to apply.

Proving Your Point!

Young children and adolescents are often heard to respond to the question "Why?" with "Because!" and little else. Another essential test-taking skill is being able to prove your point of view in a variety of ways.

FIGURE 6.12   Items That Require Students to Take a Stand on Content

Science

According to the article provided, what is the cause of changes in the exercisers? What other factors, not mentioned in the article, could account for the results? In your response, be sure to give two alternative explanations that could account for the increase in muscle size and strength.

Mathematics

Amy has test scores of 75, 89, 94, and 86 from four 100-point tests. The final exam counts as two tests and therefore is worth 200 points. Can Amy bring her average up to 90 percent when she takes the final exam? If so, what score must she get? If not, explain why not. Provide a complete explanation to show how you arrived at your answer.

Source: Michigan High School Test.

An important idea here is that students need to make connections between the stands they take and the evidence they need to provide. A related idea is that not all kinds of evidence are appropriate in every situation. Evidence for a position can come from at least several sources, including real-life observations and/or experiences and content-specific knowledge. However, students do not automatically understand how to judge which evidence is appropriate for a given situation.

Although this skill appears to be simple, it actually involves a number of important steps. First, students need to understand what it means to take a stand and how a statement of opinion or perspective is different from supporting ideas or details. Second, students need to know what it means to support an opinion or perspective. Finally, students need to know which kinds of support to provide, from general to specific prior knowledge to different aspects of content knowledge. Ways to help students develop these understandings are covered in the next chapter.

Applying the Processes of Selection and Elimination

These skills are perhaps the least useful of the test-taking skills, but because they are so prevalent in high-stakes multiple-choice tests, they are included here. Multiple-choice tests are often constructed by first creating the question or stem and then devising the choices for the item. In my experience, the writers of multiple-choice items usually indentify the correct answer first. Often, they then create an answer that is the direct opposite of the correct answer. The final incorrect selections are crafted by identifying minor, inconsequential, or even ludicrous details. I have observed this pattern on tests for English, science, and social studies.

The process played out in mathematics is a bit different, though similar. The correct answer is there, but the incorrect answers are usually numbers or operations *on the way to* the correct answer.

$$(x + 4)(x - 3)$$

Which expression indicates the outcome of multiplying the two terms above?

   a. $x^2 + x - 12$
   b. $4x - 3x$
   c. -12
   d. $2x + 1$

The final choice here represents a common student misconception with regard to this problem, where students add the terms, rather than multiplying as the problem requires. It also illustrates that many multiple-choice items are dependent on students knowing something about the content on which they are being tested.

Having the right kinds of content knowledge is important for answering most multiple-choice items in mathematics, science, and social studies.

What, then, are some strategies to help students with these kinds of assessment? The strategy known as the **process of selection** is the idea that if a student has a hunch that an answer is the right one, the information should appear somewhere in the test material. This is especially true for tests that involve narrative or informational passages. Because the item writers select information directly from these passages, a correct answer will represent a match or near-match with the passage information. The message here for students is simple: If you think you have the right answer, scan the reading material for the test and make sure the answer appears somewhere in the reading. (Note that this strategy will not work in cases where an answer requires specific kinds of content knowledge.)

Applying the **process of elimination** is a skill that many of us discovered through our own testing experiences: Eliminate incorrect answers until only one or two remain. It may surprise you how many students do not understand this skill. A discussion of how this works, along with some examples, can be a simple way to help students become more familiar with multiple choice tests.

Integrating Essential Test-Taking Skills into the Curriculum

I believe that when teachers emphasize these skills, students not only do better on high-stakes tests but also learn skills that are extremely valuable later in life. The problem of how to integrate these skills into the curriculum remains. How to do this is the topic of the next chapter.

SPECIAL PROJECTS

For Beginning Teachers

Figure 6.13 depicts a set of ethical standards for test taking from one state. What test preparation practices are encouraged? Which are discouraged? Discuss your philosophy about striking a balance between teaching valued curriculum concepts and test preparation.

For Experienced Teachers

Consider the essential test-taking skills outlined in this chapter. Describe some ways in which you could incorporate these skills into your own teaching.

FIGURE 6.13   Ethical Standards for Test Preparation and Administration

Test Preparation Standards

There are several different ways to prepare students to do well on the tests. When judged by standards of fairness and students' long-term retention of knowledge and skills, some ways are considered more appropriate than others. In general, activities that promote quality, long-term learning are appropriate. Unethical and inappropriate activities are those aimed only at increasing short-term learning and test scores.

Any classroom, school, or district found to have carried out unethical or inappropriate activities may have its scores invalidated, and its summary scores reported as zeros.

The following lists detail…inappropriate activities for test preparation.
It is *unethical* or *inappropriate* to:

- administer the tests without first notifying both the students and parents.
- review *only* tested skills, strategies, and concepts. This includes reviewing only those areas in which student performance was low on previous tests.
- "cram" tested materials just before the tests are given.
- alter test questions and use them for practice.
- review or provide answers to test questions.
- administer an excessive number of practice tests.
- use current or past test items.
- use computer software, worksheets, and other published materials to drill students just on tested skills, strategies, and concepts.
- reveal, copy, or otherwise reproduce test questions or student responses in any manner, oral or written.
- possess unauthorized copies of tests.

Test Administration Standards

It is *unethical* or *inappropriate* to:

- read any parts of the tests to students, except where indicated in the directions.
- give special help of any kind to students taking the tests.
- suggest or coach students to mark or change their answers in any way.
- define and/or pronounce words used in the test (except as indicated in the directions).
- erase or change student answers.
- have students revisit answers after a testing session is completed.
- display materials in classrooms that would unfairly advantage students who see them during testing over students who do not.

SUGGESTED READINGS

Popham, W. J. (2001). *Classroom assessment: What teachers need to know.* New York: Allyn and Bacon.
Stiggins, R. (2005). *Student-involved assessment FOR learning.* Columbus, OH: Merrill Prentice Hall.

7 Building Lessons around Test-Taking Skills That Matter

How to Promote Learning of the Essential Test-Taking Skills

This chapter presents lesson ideas for using and applying the essential test-taking skills with your students.

Understanding and Distinguishing between Big and Small Ideas

Big ideas are found in all of the content areas. These are ideas that both make up and organize the content areas. Many of the big ideas are in content area standards, in the form of broad, general statements about content, such as those shown in Figure 7.1. Big ideas are also found on tests in the form of correct answers on multiple-choice tests. On some tests, all of the answers are big ideas, but only one of the answers—the correct one—represents the *most* information from a reading passage (see Figure 7.2). Big ideas are commonly found in the form of writing prompts for almost any test; Figure 7.3 offers an example.

How can we help students find their way among the big ideas, distinguishing between appropriate and inappropriate ideas, as well as determining relationships between big ideas and small, concepts, and details? Consider the following teaching ideas.

It can be difficult for students to understand the difference between big and small ideas, especially when they are contained in text. A helpful strategy is to introduce an analogy from the real world that uses the idea of different sizes. For instance, consider using the human hand (see Figure 7.4). Each finger can represent a smaller idea, while the entire hand stands for a big idea. Each finger contributes to the bigger idea expressed on the palm. Once students get accustomed to this analogy, they can fill out their own hands (traced on a piece of paper, of course!) with a big idea of their own, such as pets, places they have visited, or favorite friends, and note its relationship to the smaller ideas they list on their drawings' fingers.

FIGURE 7.1   Big Ideas in the Content Areas, from the California Content Standards

Mathematics

Number sense

Students compare and order positive and negative fractions, decimals, and mixed numbers. Students solve problems involving fractions, ratios, proportions, and percentages.

Science

Structure of Matter

Students know that compounds are formed by combining two or more different elements and that compounds have properties that are different from their constituent elements.

Social Studies

Geography

Students demonstrate an understanding of the physical and human geographic features that define places and regions in California.

Language Arts

Comprehension and Analysis of Grade-Level-Appropriate Text

Identify and trace the development of an author's argument, point of view, or perspective in text.

FIGURE 7.2   Big Ideas in a Multiple-Choice Item

This story is MOSTLY ABOUT

1. How a woman learns to live with the misunderstandings of outsiders.   ←
2. How a woman learns to honor her father.
3. How a woman learns to be a good student.
4. How a woman learns to set up a booth at the county fair.

After these kinds of activities, it is time to transfer students' understandings to text examples, such as the passages given in Figure 7.5. To find other passages with which to get across the idea of big and small, look through the students' classroom books or visit popular news websites, such as those of the Associated Press (*www.ap.org*), NBC News (*www.msnbc.com*), USA Today (*www.usatoday.com*), and Fox News (*www.foxnews.com*).

These websites often contain short, easy-to-read passages on a variety of interesting topics. These passages can be quite useful in helping students see the differences between large, topical ideas and smaller ideas and details.

To work with these passages, select from a number of possible exercises such as the following:

FIGURE 7.3   Big Ideas Within Writing Prompts

Writing (People's Differences)

In dealing with peoples' differences, some people choose to be insensitive or hurtful or they try to better understand others and build good relationships based on differences. **Write a paper in which you examine how you think people should view and use others' differences in their daily lives.**

You might, for example, do one of the following:

explain why differences that you think are important may not be as important for someone else

OR

consider a time when you felt people's differences were ignored

OR

examine whether television or movies treat people's differences seriously

OR

Take any of several other approaches to discussing this idea

Your audience will be interested adult readers.

Social Studies (Individual Rights versus the Rights of Society)

You will now take a stand on the following public policy issue: Should the state legislature require student athletes to take random, mandatory tests for illegal and/or performance-enhancing drugs? You may either support or oppose student athletes being required to take these tests for drugs.

Write a letter to your state representative. Use information to provide reasons that support your position.

Mathematics (How Area Applies to Real-Life Situations)

In order to re-seed their lawn, Martel's mother got two estimates. The Greenery would charge a flat fee of $750. The Lawn Shop would charge 10¢ per square foot.

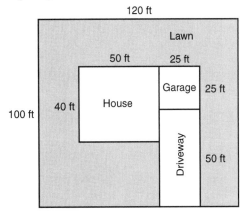

What is the **LEAST** expensive estimate? Explain your answer and compute the savings resulting from the difference in prices.

Science (Pollution and the Ecosystem)

A company wants to build a factory to produce weed killer. The new factory will be located close to the lake ecosystem with the food web shown in the diagram above. [We omit the diagram.] What would happen if weed killer from the factory were to pollute the lake? In your response, be sure to include two ways the aquatic food chain could be affected.

Source: Michigan Educational Assessment Program.

- Fill out a "big and small ideas" hand for the passage.
- Underline the biggest idea in the passage.
- Cut up the passage into individual sentences and arrange the ideas from biggest to smallest.
- Create a map of the big and small ideas in each passage.

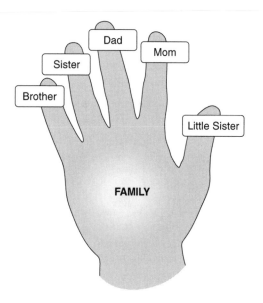

FIGURE 7.4   Using a Hand to Illustrate Big and Small Ideas

FIGURE 7.5   Sample Passages for Working with Big and Small Ideas

The Crocodile Hunter

The crocodile hunter on television is a big risk taker. His name is Steve Irwin. He lives in Australia. Last week, he wrestled an alligator. Next week, he is supposed to try to outrun a Komodo dragon, one of the largest living lizards. I've even seen him crawl into a cave with seven rattlesnakes.

Space Vehicles

There are just a small number of vehicles that have been especially made for space travel. One vehicle is the rocket. Rockets carry small capsules, such as the Gemini, the Apollo, and the Soyuz. The space shuttle was created to as a vehicle that could fly in space and in Earth's gravity. The lunar rover was invented for travel on the moon.

Harry Potter Books

So far, J. K. Rowling has written five best-selling and popular Harry Potter books. The first book is *Harry Potter and the Sorcerer's Stone.* The second book is *Harry Potter and the Chamber of Secrets,* and the third book is *Harry Potter and the Prisoner of Azkaban.* These books have already been made into popular movies. The fourth book is *Harry Potter and the Goblet of Fire.* My favorite book, is the fifth book, *Harry Potter and the Order of the Phoenix.*

FIGURE 7.6 Examples of News Stories for Finding Big and Small Ideas

Mix-up Dooms Mars Probe

A mix-up over metric and English measurements likely caused the loss of the $125-million Mars Climate Orbiter as it started to circle the planet last week, officials said Thursday. The error caused the probe to fly too close to the red planet, causing the spacecraft to break up or burn up in the Martian atmosphere that it had been designed to study, mission controllers at NASA's Jet Propulsion Laboratory said. Laboratory officials said their preliminary findings showed that Lockheed Martin Astronautics in Colorado submitted acceleration data in English units of pounds of force instead of in the metric units called newtons. At the laboratory, the numbers were entered into a computer that assumed metric measurements. Quality control failed to notice the discrepancy. The bad numbers had been used ever since the spacecraft's launch last December, but the effect was so small that it went unnoticed. The difference added up over the months as the spacecraft journeyed toward Mars.

Venus Williams Is Back!

Venus Williams looked rejuvenated from a six-month layoff. Williams returned at the Australian Open and needed less than an hour to beat American teenager Ashley Harkleroad 6–2, 6–1 on Tuesday in a first-round match. The third-seeded Williams was very focused on Melbourne Park's center court. She showed no rust—and no signs of the abdominal injury that sidelined her—while serving at speeds up to 119 mph. Venus is back now, and competitors better beware. Williams's only slips were a twisted ankle in the fourth game and one dropped service game, in the fifth game of the second set.

For the last idea, creating a map, guide students in finding the biggest idea in the passage. Then help them determine which are the smaller ideas. Figure 7.7 depicts one way of doing this for the story about the Mars probe. As you may notice, there are a number of ways to construct this map. Some students may wish to put the orbiter's demise at the center. Other students may wish to put the miscalculations at the center. Either approach is fine, as long as the students can defend their choices.

Analyzing Questions

One of the best recommendations from experts on assessment is to get into the habit of analyzing, with students, what it will take to be successful in any of the classroom assignments they are asked to complete (Wiggins 1998; Stiggins 2005). This practice alone can go a long way toward helping students do better not only in their daily work but also on various kinds of assessment. A simple way to illustrate this is to consider giving students an essay assignment, such as this one: **Write a letter to the principal convincing him or her that a school rule is fair or unfair.**

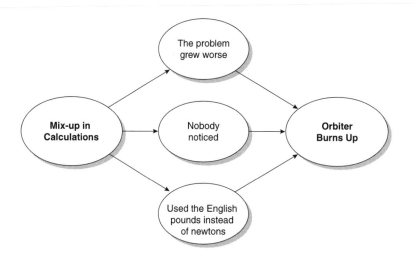

FIGURE 7.7   **A Map of Text, Demonstrating Big and Small Ideas**

After presenting this as an assignment, ask, "How would we know that we had written a successful essay?" This question addresses the issue of the qualities desired for the essay. Possible answers: a business letter format is chosen, the principal is clearly the audience, the tone is respectful, a school rule is mentioned, and an opinion is given along with supporting reasons.

> **To help students analyze questions, ask**
> What is a good response to this question?
> How many parts are there to this question?
> What are the expectations for what I need to produce to answer this question?

Following this example is a way to help students begin to understand what it means to produce quality work in response to a question, assignment, or task they are assigned. Many students are unaccustomed to taking this preparatory step, preferring instead to barrel through questions impatiently, without pausing to discover what a question or assignment is actually asking. Often, this means that students miss important aspects of a question, such as the real substance of the question and whether or not it calls for multiple responses.

Consider the question shown in Figure 7.8, which is not unlike many found on a variety of math assessments. How many parts are there in the question? Two? Three? There are actually three parts: writing a question, creating an answer, and offering an explanation. Note that the test provides only two places for responses, one for a question and one for an answer. To help with this problem—the multipart question—have students circle or underline or number each individual part. That way, they will be in a position to receive full credit, or at least try to earn full credit.

FIGURE 7.8   **Helping Students Analyze a Mathematics Question**

Mathematics

Write one question that uses information provided in the following table. Give the correct answer to your question. Also, explain why the answer you gave is correct.

Altitude (in feet)	Wind Direction and Speed (in miles per hour)	Temperature (in degrees centigrade)
3,000	West at 12	$0°$
6,000	Northwest at 22	Minus $6°$
9,000	North at 24	Minus $12°$
12,000	East at 50	Minus $18°$

Question:

Answer:

What exactly, is this question calling for? This is an unusual question in that it is not asking directly for a response. Rather, in the *Jeopardy* game show fashion, it is asking for a question! Then it calls for a response. This activity is actually more difficult than answering a question directly. Practice with asking questions would probably help many students succeed with this type of test question.

How do students successfully answer this question? They must use information from the chart. Note that students could ask relatively easy questions whose answers are derived directly from the chart: "How cold is it at 9000 feet? Minus 12 degrees." But if they wander into explanations that have no answer on the chart, such as "*Why does it get colder as the altitude increases?*", they may not receive full credit. Careful modeling of how to take questions apart and figure out how to respond will help many students become more comfortable and in control of their responses to classroom and assessment tasks.

Getting Organized

Getting organized is another area where students falter, in part because they do not know what is required of them on assessments, but also because they do not know how to get started in responding to a question or how to organize their responses.

One important rule is to start answering a question by *referring directly to the question itself*. More specifically, it is essential to use language from a question to start answering the question. Consider the following essay assignment: **Take a**

stand on whether or not the media—television, music, and movies—encourage violence. You can get them thinking by presenting three or four different ways to begin their response, such as

1. Violent movies are the best!
2. The only good movies have kissing in them.
3. I hate Britney Spears.
4. I think television encourages violence because…

Students will probably see that the most direct response is the last one. The others offer opinions but say little about the question itself.

Another part of getting organized is working out a structure, map, or diagram for what you want to say. Sometimes this means just making a simple list of things to say. Other responses might require more sophistication, involving patterns of ideas, such as comparisons, problem and solutions, or cause and effect. Each of these situations calls for specific teaching about the patterns in the context of different kinds of questions or assignments.

FIGURE 7.9   Helping Students Chart Their Response to a Question

Kinds of Pollution	Impact on the Environment
Toxic liquids, chemical waste	Seep into the groundwater, contaminate drinking water
Factory and car emissions	Foul the air, create health problems
Insulating materials	Release toxic gasses into residences and businesses
Litter and trash	Create unsightly mess, foul the water, land, and air (from decay and burning)

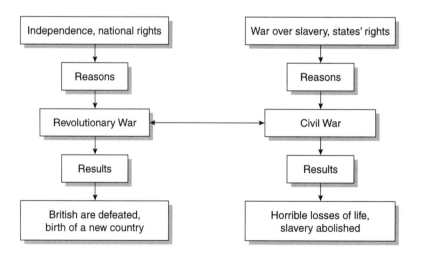

FIGURE 7.10   Mapping Out a Response to a Question, Using Comparisons

For instance, when asked to consider the impact of different kinds of pollution on the environment, students might create the diagram shown in Figure 7.9 to help them answer. The underlying pattern is cause and effect.

Other ways of getting organized might entail drawing a semantic map. *Semantic maps* are simply diagrams that depict relationships among ideas. Consider the map shown in Figure 7.10, which was produced in response to the following question: **Compare the Revolutionary War with the Civil War.** There are many, many different ways to sketch out an answer to a question. Think about some ways in which you organize your responses to questions. More than likely, you will come up with some additional ways to help students get organized for responding to various questions and assignments.

Thinking about What You Already Know

Many students rush into responding to questions without considering what they already know. Have you ever experienced a time when you completed a test, walked out, and then suddenly remembered what you should have said? Thinking about what you know ahead of time might have helped.

There are a number of strategies for helping students get into the habit of thinking about what they know before responding. One popular strategy is K–W–L, a strategy used in reading but useful in a variety of subject areas (Ogle 1986). In this strategy (see Figure 7.11), students are guided in thinking about what they already know about a topic, they ask questions about what they want to learn, and then they respond to those questions on the basis of readings or other experiences (Web-based

FIGURE 7.11 The K–W–L Procedure to Help Students Think about What They Already Know

K What I *Know*	W What I *Want* to Learn	L What I Have *Learned*

searches, library searches, and so on). It is a mistake to assume that students already know how to apply these strategies (Conley 1995). Although the chart is simple, which is an advantage, students will still need you to guide them carefully through its use, modeling each of the steps until they are able to think on their own about what they know.

Taking a Stand on Content

Students usually have opinions—even convictions—about things, but they do not always know how to apply them responsibly, especially in testing situations. As a result, helping students learn to take reasoned, responsible stands can be a big benefit to them.

To get started, offer students a list of topics about which someone could offer an opinion. Ask, "What do you think? What do you believe? How do you feel about that? Is it right? Is it wrong?" Figure 7.12 gives a list of topics you may wish to consider for this exercise.

Key Questions to Promote Taking a Stand

What do you think?
What do you believe?
How do you feel about that?
Is that a correct answer?
Is that right? Is it wrong?

Once students are accustomed to coming up with their own points of view, it is important to help them distinguish points of view from facts. Many students, when confronted with a big idea on a writing assignment or test, produce lists of facts without connecting them to a point of view. Solving this problem starts with an exercise such as the one in Figure 7.13.

FIGURE 7.12   Topics that Lend Themselves to Taking a Stand

What Do You Think About...?

Parents' rules	The criminal justice system
Racy television shows	Crooked politicians
Violent video games	Wars overseas
Overpaid athletes	Drunk driving laws

FIGURE 7.13   Distinguishing Points of View from Facts

Only one of the following is a point of view. For each question, circle the answer that is the best example of a point of view.

Question 1:

a) Girls should have the same rights as boys.
b) Our school sits on a corner.
c) Cars can go fast or slow.
d) Our hamster eats raw corn.

Question 2:

a) The Detroit Tigers are the worst team in baseball.
b) There are nine players in the outfield.
c) The pitcher stands on a mound.
d) There are four bases in the field.

Question 3:

a) Teachers should never have favorite students.
b) There are twenty-five students in this class.
c) Gina wears a red sweater.
d) The computers stopped working yesterday.

Proving Your Point!

Now the difficult work begins! Teaching students to prove what they say can be a big challenge, because they need to know not only how to support their points of view but also how to provide the right *kinds* of support, which can range from background experience all the way to specific kinds of content knowledge.

> **Key Questions to Promote Reasons and Evidence**
>
> How do you know that?
> Point that out to me.
> Why? Why not?
> Where does that answer come from?
> Show me where it says that.
> What are the facts that support that?

To get started on this skill, work on promoting habits of mind in students by regularly asking, "How do you know that? What are your reasons for saying/

writing that? What are the facts that support what you are saying/writing?" Once students have responded to "How do you know that?" or "Show me how you know that" enough times, they usually start proving their point of view on their own. This single habit can pay big dividends on the tests that students take and in their everyday reasoning.

Early on, students need to understand just how to support a point of view with particular kinds of evidence. The exercises in Figure 7.14 will help students learn how to connect points of view with factual evidence. Next, have students generate their own reasons and details, with respect to points of view, as in the exercises given in Figures 7.15 and 7.16. Note that the exercise in Figure 7.17 requires more independence on the part of students. Organize exercises such as these in ways that help students gradually build their understanding of what it means to provide evidence and support for their positions. One way to do this is to have students work first with general background knowledge, including facts and details, and then move on to exercises that emphasize content knowledge, as in Figure 7.17.

FIGURE 7.14   Connecting Points of View with Facts

Directions: Some facts go better with a point of view than others. Circle the facts in the list that have the most to do with the point of view.

Point of View

SUVs are more harmful to the environment than other cars.

Facts

SUVs only get 17 miles per gallon.
My uncle owns a Honda.
Cars that get low mileage pollute the air more than other cars.
SUV owners get in more car crashes than other drivers.

Directions: Using the following facts, circle the point of view that best summarizes the facts.

Facts

The state of Michigan is short 1.8 million dollars for next year's state budget.
This past Christmas, people purchased fewer presents than in previous years.
Some companies have started to slow down production and to lay off workers.

Points of View

The economy is off to a running start for the year.
The economy is in a downturn and, so far, shows no signs of improving.
My uncle Fred is a pipe fitter.

FIGURE 7.15 Taking a Stand and Backing It Up

Question

Should people who hurt animals be treated the same way as if they hurt a human being?

Taking My Stand!

I believe that *animals should have the same rights as humans.* _____

Why? 1 Animals are our best friends.

Fact 1 _____

Fact 2 _____

Fact 3 _____

Why? 2 Animals have feelings and experience pain just like we do.

Fact 1 _____

Fact 2 _____

Fact 3 _____

Why? 3 If we treat animals the right way, they will treat us the right way.

Fact 1 _____

Fact 2 _____

Fact 3 _____

FIGURE 7.16 Taking a Stand and Backing It Up

Question

Should our city allow more shopping malls to be built?

Taking My Stand!

I believe that _____

_____

Why? 1 Shopping malls give people more jobs.

_____

_____

Why? 2 _____

_____

Why? 3 _____

_____

FIGURE 7.17   **Taking a Stand and Backing It Up with Content Knowledge, Facts, and Details**

Mathematics Question:

What is the best way to figure out how much it would cost to paint your bedroom?

Taking My Stand!

The best way to figure out how much it would cost to paint my bedroom is _____

_____

_____

Supporting Fact: I need to figure the area of the room.

Example: _____

Supporting Fact: One can of paint covers 400 square feet.

Supporting Fact: One can of paint costs $11.99.

Supporting Fact: It will take nearly two cans of paint to cover my room.

Social Studies Question:

What is the cause of most of the wars that have been fought by the United States?

Taking My Stand!

Most wars fought by the United States have been fought for economic reasons.

Supporting Example 1: The Revolutionary War was sparked by disputes with England over trade and taxes.

Supporting Example 2: The Civil War was caused by conflict between the industrialized North and the rural South.

Supporting Example 3: Some people argue that the recent wars in the Middle East were caused by disputes over the price of oil.

Applying the Processes of Selection and Elimination

As we noted in Chapter 6, skills such as applying the process of selection and the process of elimination may be the least productive skills, at least as far as the classroom curriculum is concerned. These skills are needed almost exclusively on multiple-choice tests and are rarely, if ever, needed in other areas of school or in life. Most educators rightly resist turning their entire curriculum over to emphasis on these test-taking skills. However, a certain amount of familiarity with these skills is useful and helps students feel more at home in the test-taking environment.

Consider employing released items and other published test preparation materials to develop these skills in students. Many teachers report the benefits of some advance rehearsal with these materials before students take high-stakes and other kinds of tests with multiple-choice formats. Talk with your students about how multiple-choice items are constructed. Help them gain an "insider's perspective" about how item writers scan texts for real and plausible answers. Talk with your students about the following strategies, particularly with respect to what to do once one sees a possible answer.

- Eliminate obviously wrong answers.
- Scan the text involved for correct or even word-for-word references to specific item choices.
- Once a correct answer is identified, scan the text for confirmation that the answer is indeed correct.

Combine the strategies discussed throughout this chapter with these test-taking skills to produce the greatest impact not only on tests but also on students' engagement with the curriculum.

SPECIAL PROJECT

For Beginning Teachers

Select one of the test-taking skills described in this chapter and explain how you would create an activity in which a student could learn that skill.

For Experienced Teachers

Design some instructional activities for the assessment skills described in this chapter.

SUGGESTED READINGS

Readence, J., Moore, D., & Rickelman, R. (2000). *Prereading activities for content area reading and learning.* Newark, DE: International Reading Association.

Vacca, R., & Vacca, J. (2002). *Content area reading: Literacy and learning across the curriculum.* New York: Addison-Wesley.

Wood, K., & Harmon, J. (2000). *Strategies for integrating reading and writing in middle and high school classrooms.* Newark, DE: International Reading Association.

8 Integrating Standards and Assessment through Daily Practice

How to create lessons that come from thinking about both the standards and the test-taking skills needed for performance on large- and small-scale tests

In this chapter, we will take up the challenge faced by many educators in this new era: creating instruction and assessment that build from the standards *and* the essential test-taking skills.

Steps for Integrated Lesson Planning

Select a standard
Select a test-taking skill.
Identify a teaching activity.
Brainstorm what teaching and learning will look like.

Designing and Teaching Integrated Lessons

As discussed in an earlier chapter, many educators approach the task of implementing standards and teaching responsibly to test-taking skills the hard way. They try to tackle all of the standards at once or to integrate standards and assessment skills all at once. The approach to integrating standards and assessments here will be a simple one: Select a single standard; select a single, related test-taking skill; identify appropriate teaching practices; and brainstorm what teaching and learning will look like. Each of these steps is described in this section.

The first task is to select related standards and test-taking skills. To do this, it might be helpful to organize in chart form your standards and the essential test-taking skills discussed in the last chapter. Figures 8.1, 8.2, 8.3, and 8.4 depict the standards from one state's curriculum framework, organized in a chart for each subject area, in relation to each of the test-taking skills. This approach makes it easier to see natural relationships between standards and test-taking skills.

For instance, in reading and language arts, the topic of understanding enduring themes in literature fits very nicely with test-taking skills such as thinking

FIGURE 8.1   Assessment Skills and Reading/Language Arts Standards

	Comprehending and Composing	Using Language Effectively	Language as a Tool	Reading, Writing, Speaking, Listening	Multiple Genre	Understanding Voice and Style
Distinguishing between Big and Small Ideas						
Analyzing Questions						
Getting Organized						
Thinking about What You Already Know						
Taking a Stand on Content						
Proving Your Point!						
Applying the Processes of Selection and Elimination						

(continued)

FIGURE 8.1 Continued

	Strategies for Making Meaning	Enduring Themes	Applying Ideas in Action	Characteristics of Texts	Inquiry and Research	Critical Thinking
Distinguishing between Big and Small Ideas						
Analyzing Questions						
Getting Organized						
Thinking about What You Already Know						
Taking a Stand on Content						
Proving Your Point!						
Applying the Processes of Selection and Elimination						

FIGURE 8.2   Assessment Skills and Mathematics Standards7

	Patterns, Relationships, and Functions	Geometry and Measurement	Data Analysis and Statistics	Number Sense and Numeration	Numerical and Algebraic Operations, Analytical Thinking	Probability and Discrete Mathematics
Distinguishing between Big and Small Ideas						
Analyzing Questions						
Getting Organized						
Thinking about What You Already Know						
Taking a Stand on Content						
Proving Your Point!						
Applying the Processes of Selection and Elimination						

FIGURE 8.3 Assessment Skills and Science Standards

	Earth, Life, and Physical Sciences	Use Scientific Knowledge to Solve Real-World Problems	Construct New Scientific Knowledge through Research, Reading, and Discussion	Demonstrate Familiarity with the Natural World	Make Informed Judgments on Statements Claiming to have a Scientific Basis	Reflect in an Informed Way on the Role of Science in Human Affairs
Distinguishing between Big and Small Ideas						
Analyzing Questions						
Getting Organized						
Thinking about What You Already Know						
Taking a Stand on Content						
Proving Your Point!						
Applying the Processes of Selection and Elimination						

FIGURE 8.4   Assessment Skills and Social Studies Standards

	Use Knowledge of the Past to Understand Our Cultural Heritage and Make Civic Judgments	Use Knowledge of Geography and How It Shapes the Human Environment	Use Knowledge of Government and Politics to Make Decisions about Governing the Local Community	Use Knowledge of Economics to Make Personal, Career, and Societal Decisions	Use Methods of Social Science Inquiry to Answer Questions about Society	Construct Thoughtful Positions on Public Issues	Act Constructively to Further the Public Good
Distinguishing between Big and Small Ideas							
Analyzing Questions							
Getting Organized							
Thinking about What You Already Know							
Taking a Stand on Content							
Proving Your Point!							
Applying the Processes of Selection and Elimination							

about what you know, taking a stand on content, and proving your point. As statements of human values or conditions, themes in literature are applicable to our lives in a variety of ways. A goal in teaching to this standard is often to help students see relationships between literary themes and their lives. It is relatively easy to envision lesson activities that help students think about what they know or have experienced with respect to a theme, take a perspective, and back it up on the basis of their experiences and readings. Charting the standards and test-taking skills thus becomes a way of brainstorming activities that bring the standards and test-taking skills together.

Let's consider another example. In the chart depicting the mathematics standards (Figure 8.2), the topic "Patterns, Relationships, and Functions" fits together nicely with the test-taking skills "Distinguishing between Big and Small Ideas" and "Getting Organized." An instructional activity that pulls this standard and these skills together involves the study of tessellations. Tessellations are formed by arranging the same figure, such as a triangle or a square, over and over again, such that a larger pattern is created. The classic example of a tessellation is a beehive. Bee-

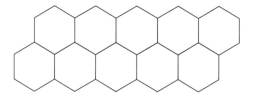

hives are composed of thousands of identical hexagons. Mosaics are also frequently composed of smaller figures that *tessellate*, or form a checkered or tiling pattern. Teachers need to familiarize students with tessellations through multiple examples, including those developed by the Dutch artist M. C. Escher. Then students can create their own designs, developing their understanding of big and small and of organization in the context of geometric forms. Again, the standards and assessment skills chart serves as a brainstorming device for designing integrated lessons.

Next let's develop a lesson, using the chart depicting the science standards and essential test-taking skills (Figure 8.3). Many young children and adolescents are concerned with the environment, even though they may not yet understand how ecosystems work or grasp the fragility of plants and animals in different ecosystems. Consequently, let's select the standard that focuses on using scientific knowledge to solve real-world problems. The real-world problem we will tackle concerns the destruction of old-growth forests. Old-growth forests are over 250 years old and contain large trees (over 100 feet tall and 6.5 feet in diameter) as well as big fallen logs and thick undergrowth. Old-growth forests are extremely desirable habitats for animal species that are nearly extinct, such as the spotted owl. However, such forests produce the best lumber and thus are also prime logging grounds. Scientists and politicians are divided within their ranks about harvesting old-growth forests.

Exploring this topic lends itself to work with test-taking skills, such as analyzing questions, taking a stand on content, and proving your point. Students first need to consider carefully key questions in the debate over old-growth forests:

- Are animals within old-growth forests worthy of survival?
- Should efforts to ensure the survival of endangered species be allowed to hinder economic development?
- Do young forests contribute to the ecosystem in ways that are similar to old-growth forests?
- Should lumber harvesting in old-growth forests be banned?

Just asking the questions a certain way can bias the entire debate.

Taking a stand on this issue undoubtedly requires reading and research via library books and other print resources or even via the Internet. Instruction in conducting this kind of research and guidance in critically reflecting on the scientific content of these resources are a must. And students need to understand how to use their research to support unambiguously the positions they take on the issue.

Finally, let's consider how to craft a lesson using the social studies standards and the essential test-taking skills. In this case, we will select the standards topic of how geography shapes the human environment. More specifically, the focus will be on helping younger children in Michigan learn more about their local community, why people settled there, and the way the local geography influences how people work and play. The setting is Michigan, where the Grand River connects Detroit to Lansing and then to Grand Rapids. Each community originally grew because of the Grand River. The river connected the communities for commerce and served as a source of water power. One could argue that there would be no Detroit, Lansing, or Grand Rapids without the Grand River having created a place for people to work and play. To this day, the Grand River functions as a recreational center for boating, fishing, and swimming.

Not surprisingly, many students have not considered the implications of living near the Grand River, historically or personally. As a result, the test-taking skill most useful here is thinking about what you already know. A lesson that integrates geography with students' knowledge might begin with the question "Why are there such large communities, like Detroit, Lansing, and Grand Rapids, located on the Grand River?" Subsequent questions might focus on the kinds of manufacturing going on in those locations, both historically and in modern times. Students could research and read about the development of communities and commerce along the Grand River to build their understandings of the river in their own backyards.

As each of these examples illustrates, many possibilities for teaching and learning emerge when the relationships between standards and the essential test-taking skills are considered. By charting these standards and skills in your area, you can create a fairly simple yet powerful approach to integrating standards and test-taking skills within the same lessons and units of study.

Revising and Redesigning Published Materials

We can use the same type of charting procedure to revise and redesign published materials. Each year, it seems that publishers create a stampede to keep up with the latest standards-based terminology or to give the appearance of producing instructional materials consistent with the latest tests. Far too often, this takes the form of merely changing labels for questions and activities to conform to standards and assessments, whether or not the activities presented truly reflect those goals.

This time, we will start with the published materials. A number of publishers of materials for early readers prepare units of study organized around different ways of telling the story of the three little pigs. For example, one story, *The Three Little Wolves and the Big Bad Pig,* reverses the roles (Oxenbury 1997). Another story, *The True Story of the Three Little Pigs,* takes a newspaper tabloid approach to the story, with the big bad wolf claiming that he was framed (Scieszka 1996). And, of course, there is the traditional fable.

In attempting to please everyone, publishers might try to combine any or all of the following:

- vocabulary and spelling activities
- setting personal learning goals
- story writing, descriptive and persuasive writing
- story structure and summarizing
- grammar and sentence work
- background readings, including poetry and informational texts
- integrating other subjects, including science (Just how hard did the wolf blow?), mathematics (Just how much did those pigs weigh?), and social studies (Did the wolf really deserve society's scorn?)
- evaluating fantasy and reality
- self-assessment, classroom assessment

Although they are well intentioned, the shear number and range of these activities can be overwhelming. More important, it becomes difficult at best to consider standards and high-stakes assessments in the context of the publisher's plan and design.

This is where charting the standards and essential test-taking skills becomes most useful. Consider the reading and language arts standard that emphasizes enduring themes. Some teachers' editions focus on the humorous structure of the three little pigs sagas, but the enduring theme that unites them all concerns the big idea of good people and bad people. There are a number of ways of thinking about this theme with the three little pigs in mind. Here are a few:

- In the animal world too, there can be good guys and bad guys.
- Sometimes certain animals, such as pigs and wolves, can get an undeserved bad reputation.
- People (and animals too) can change their ways.

Working within this intersection of enduring themes and big ideas, teacher can now select, ignore, or adapt publishers' activities, the overall goal being to help students work with a literary theme while taking a stand on some of the big ideas within the three little pigs story alternatives. With this focus in mind, word study, comprehension, writing, and activities related to test taking can be evaluated with regard to how well they will help students achieve the integrated goals of the lesson.

To recap, modifying published materials in terms of standards and the essential test-taking skills starts by examining the materials for an overall focus and range of activities. Use the standards and assessment skills charts, modified for the standards and assessments in your area, to select, revise, and supplement what the publishers provide. Finally, select or redesign tests so that they are more consistent with your integrated focus on standards and assessment skills.

Creating Opportunities for Reading, Writing, and Reasoning

Integrating standards and essential test-taking skills can also mean creating opportunities for reading, writing, and reasoning. Again, we can use charts that

FIGURE 8.5   Standards, Big Ideas, and Essential Test-Taking Skills to Stimulate Reading

Standards-Based Big Ideas	Essential Test-Taking Skills
Science	
Why does it sometimes feel colder when the temperature is 30 degrees than when it is below zero? (humans in the natural world, effects of humidity)	Think about what you already know, take a stand, and prove your point.
Social Studies	
Why do some people claim that it is difficult to get justice in America? (social science inquiry)	Big and small ideas, take a stand, prove your point
Mathematics	
How much would it cost to travel overseas for vacation and live for two weeks? (mathematics, number sense)	Big and small ideas, think about what you already know, get organized, take a stand and prove your point.
English	
What would you do if you could be rich beyond your dreams? (what it means to be rich, *Brewster's Millions*, "Richard Cory")	Big and small ideas, take a stand on content, prove your point

depict the standards and test-taking skills. Where standards and skills intersect, there is considerable potential for getting students motivated and engaged to read, write, and think beyond what they are reading.

Consider the examples in Figure 8.5. On the left, there are interesting standards-based big ideas. On the right, are accompanying test-taking skills. Together, these concepts provide the basis for different kinds of reading, writing, and inquiry. For instance, the science example becomes an occasion for reading about wind chill and for interviewing parents and others about when they feel the coldest. The result could be a written report about when we feel cold, why we feel cold, and what to do about it.

The social studies example could involve students in reading about some famous cases of capital punishment and other court cases in which people were convicted but were later found to have been wrongly accused. It could also entail statistical research about crime and punishment. In the math example, students could read about exchange and per diem expense rates while they learn about other countries and the costs of living there. Finally, the English example could be an occasion for reading and writing about what it truly means to be rich, either in spirit or in cash. Note that in each of these examples, there are associated test-taking skills that can be emphasized as part of the ongoing curriculum.

SPECIAL PROJECTS

For Beginning Teachers

Using the charts in this chapter, describe how you would develop a lesson combining a standard and a test-taking skill. For example, use the standard that students should learn about enduring themes describing human experience. A theme often describes truisms about how people live their lives. Here are a few examples:

- Those who do not study the past will repeat past mistakes.
- In a war with nature, people usually do not win.
- Knowing yourself is the first step toward having true friends.

Select reading materials that you could use for a theme of your choosing. Now consider what test-taking skills would be appropriate to use with your thematic approach. Consider

- Big and small ideas
- Taking a stand
- Supporting your stand with evidence

Finally, describe how you would use your selected materials to teach students about the standard, while helping them develop some test-taking skills.

For Experienced Teachers

Create a chart like the ones depicted in this chapter in which you map out standards and test-taking skills. Using your chart or the ones in this chapter, develop a lesson that specifically involves students in reading, writing, or reasoning.

Design or revise some lessons in which you "build in" specific ways for students to gain practice with oral language and fluency.

SUGGESTED READINGS

Consult your state's curriculum standards, state assessments, and any available classroom curriculum materials for the work described in this chapter. See Appendix A for your state Department of Education website.

9 Promoting Reading Fluency

This chapter discusses reading fluency, including standards for fluency, ways of assessing fluency, and promising practices for promoting reading fluency.

In one sense, reading fluency is about smooth phrasing and expression during oral reading. Research has often demonstrated the rich connections between oral reading fluency and comprehension (Rasinski and Hoffman 2003). We know from research and practice that students who do not read well orally are likely to experience problems with comprehension. The reasons are readily understandable: When students are spending all of their time and attention focusing on the components of language—letters, sounds, syllables, words, and phrases—they have little attention left to focus on expression or to make connections that would support comprehension.

When students are not fluent, they often attend only to the segments of language with which they are familiar: letters, sounds, or familiar words. Their fragmented reading does not enable them to comprehend what they are reading. Consider this example of a child who is able to recognize the beginnings of words but hasn't quite grasped the idea of whole words:

Child's Reading	th-	p- l-	fl-	ov- ov-	th-	b- br-	ha- s
Text	The	plane	flew	over	the	brown	house.

As you can see, this child has only one basic understanding about language—that words begin with a sound. It should not come as a surprise that when asked to retell what she had just read, this child was unable to say very much. Comprehension was nearly nonexistent because of problems with oral language fluency. Many struggling readers struggle because they have not yet developed enough reading fluency to comprehend (Reutzel, Camperell, et al. 2002).

Standards in Support of Reading Fluency

Within the last several years, more and more attention has been focused on standards for reading fluency. Several research reports, including *Preventing Reading Difficulties in Young Children* (Snow, Burns, et al. 1998) and the *Report of the National Reading Panel* (National Reading Panel 2000), have emphasized the importance of reading fluency for overall reading success. Both of these rigorous reviews of scientifically based reading research have identified several understandings and skills related to language that are fundamental for developing reading fluency (National Reading Panel 2000). The research says pretty clearly that children will not become very fluent without a solid foundation in understanding and using the sounds of spoken language (phonemic awareness), along with a good grasp of the way sounds and symbols combine to make words (phonological awareness, or phonics).

Phonemic awareness is the ability to focus on and manipulate phonemes in *spoken* words. **Phonemes** are the smallest units of sounds that make up spoken language. English consists of about forty-one phonemes. Phonemes combine to form syllables and words. A few words, such as *a* and *oh*, have only one phoneme. Most words consist of a blend of phonemes, such as *go* with two phonemes, *check* with three phonemes, and *school* with four phonemes. Phonemes are not the same as letters of the alphabet, which referred to as graphemes. Phonemes are the sounds of spoken language (National Reading Panel 2000).

The following chart depicts some sample phonemes. Note that phonemes are often written as shown here to indicate that they represent spoken sounds.

Letters, or Graphemes	Phonemes
oh	/o/
go	/g/ /o/
check	/ch/ /e/ /k/
school	/s/ /k/ /u/ /l/

Phonological awareness involves an understanding of the alphabetic system, including letter–sound correspondences and spelling patterns, and the ability to apply this knowledge to reading by building and decoding words. Even though some children have an excellent grasp of phonemes, the sounds that make up spoken language, they still need to be able to relate the sounds they know in spoken language to letters—that is, to understand how letters stand for sounds—in order to be able to make the transition to reading.

In the past, many states have had only very general standards for the early elementary years, such as *All children will learn to read and comprehend by grade 3.* The trend, spurred by No Child Left Behind legislation, is to require states to be much more specific in their expectations for what should happen to support the development of fluency in the early grades. This has resulted, at the kindergarten and first grade levels particularly, in specific kinds of expectations with regard to the early development of phonemic and phonological awareness. A recent example from Minnesota is shown in Figure 9.1. Note that in this example, kindergartners are expected to develop facility mostly with phonemic awareness, whereas the emphasis in first grade is largely on building on phonemic awareness to develop phonological awareness.

FIGURE 9.1   Early Literacy Standards for Word Recognition, Analysis, and Fluency from Minnesota

Kindergarten

Standard: The student will apply knowledge of the sounds of the English language (phonemic awareness) and sound–symbol relationships (phonics).

Benchmarks

The student will:

1. See, hear, say, and write the basic sounds (phonemes) of the English language.
2. Match consonant and short vowel sounds to appropriate letters, say the common sounds of most letters, and begin to write consonant–vowel–consonant words.
3. Identify and name uppercase and lowercase letters of the alphabet.
4. Identify beginning consonant sounds and ending sounds in single-syllable words.
5. Identify, produce, and say rhyming words in response to an oral prompt.
6. Read 10 high-frequency words.

First Grade

Standard: The student will understand and apply knowledge of the sounds of the English language (phonemic awareness), the sound–symbol relationship (phonics), and word recognition strategies to read grade-level materials with accuracy and emerging fluency.

Benchmarks

The student will:

1. Identify letters, words, and sentences.
2. Match spoken words, with print.
3. See, hear, say, and write the letters, blends, and diagraphs that correspond with the common sounds of the English Language.
4. Segment and blend beginning, middle, and ending sounds (phonemes) to read unfamiliar words.
5. Divide spoken and written words into syllables and identify phonemes and phonograms within words.
6. Use letter sounds, word patterns, and parts of simple compound words to decode unfamiliar words when reading.
7. Generate rhyming words in a rhyming pattern.
8. Read 100 high-frequency words.
9. Notice when reading breaks down, reread, and use phonetic and other strategies to self-correct.
10. Read aloud grade-appropriate text with accuracy and emerging fluency.

Some states include early literacy standards for speaking and listening that apply children's developing understandings of oral and written language. Figure 9.2 lists one state's oral reading standards. The purpose here is to focus on applications of oral language that will further build children's fluency.

FIGURE 9.2   Standards for Developing Speaking and Listening

Standard: The student will communicate effectively through listening and speaking.

The student will:

1. Participate in and follow agreed-upon rules for conversation and formal discussions.
2. Follow two-step directions.
3. Attend to and understand the meaning of messages.
4. Communicate needs, feelings, and ideas to peers and adults.
5. Recite and respond to poems, rhymes, and songs.
6. Respond orally to language patterns in stories and poems.
7. Use voice level appropriate for language situation.

Fluency itself is reading with appropriate speed, accuracy, and proper expression. Just because a student builds phonemic awareness and phonological awareness does not mean that this student is completely fluent. Even when the building blocks are there, children may not have acquired enough practice or experience with spoken and written language to be fluent. As a result, there is considerable research on practices that help students put together everything they know about how language works so that they can become more fluent (Rasinski and Hoffman 2003). These practices are reviewed in the sections that follow.

Assessing Reading Fluency

There are a number of ways to determine a child's level of fluency. Many researchers now suggest that it is important to gain an understanding of how a child sees himself or herself as a reader as part of assessing reading fluency (Reutzel, Camperell, et al. 2002). A proficient reader will have a strong sense of herself or himself as a reader. Children who are good readers know when they are progressing well, and they know when they don't know something. They also have a choice of strategies from which to choose to solve a fluency problem in a particular situation: decode a sound or word, blend syllables together, combine meanings, or the like. Struggling children may not know when they are struggling—they barrel through what they can pronounce in a text, ignoring what they can't access—and they have few options when they get stuck. Using the assessments described here should help you determine which end of the continuum a child may be on—strategic versus struggling reader.

Interview questions like the following can be used as one tool for discovering a child's perspective on how she or he makes sense of language and print (Brown, Goodman, et al. 1996).

- Are you a reader?
- Do you know anyone who is a good reader? What do they do?

- What do you do when you come to something you do not know?
- What could you do to become a better reader?
- What are your favorite books? Why are they your favorites?

Responses such as "I'm not a very good reader," "When I get stuck, I don't know what to do," and "When I don't know something, I just reread it or try to memorize it" are signs that a child is struggling.

Specific tests can also be used to determine a child's abilities with phonemic awareness and phonological awareness. Note in Figure 9.3 that there are many ways to view how well a child is able to recognize, distinguish among, and manipulate sounds in spoken language.

Phonological awareness (knowledge about letter–sound relationships) is usually assessed by determining the extent to which a child can pronounce different letters, syllables, or words, as in

- Saying consonants and short vowel sounds
- Pronouncing high-frequency words (such as *a*, *the*, and *there*)
- Reading one's own name
- Blending letter patterns
- Pronouncing word families (rimes)
- Responding to spelling patterns

There are several published tests that can be used to assess early reading fluency. For instance, the Yopp–Singer test (Appendix B) is an informal, nonstandardized assessment that can be given quickly and easily to individual children.

FIGURE 9.3   Tests for Phonemic Awareness

1. **Phoneme isolation,** which requires recognizing individual sounds in words—for example, "Tell me the first sound in *paste*." (/p/)
2. **Phoneme identity,** which requires recognizing the common sound in different words—for example, "Tell me the sound that is the same in *bike, boy,* and *bell*." (/b/)
3. **Phoneme categorization,** which requires recognizing the word with the odd sound in a sequence of three or four words—for example, "Which word does not belong? *bus, bun, rug*." (*rug*)
4. **Phoneme blending,** which requires listening to a sequence of separately spoken sounds and combining them to form a recognizable word—for example, "What word is /s/ /k/ /u/ /1/?" (*school*)
5. **Phoneme segmentation,** which requires breaking a word into its sounds by tapping out or counting the sounds or by pronouncing and positioning a marker for each sound—for example, "How many phonemes are there in *ship?*" (three: /š/, /I/, and /p/)
6. **Phoneme deletion,** which requires recognizing what word remains when a specified phoneme is removed. For example, "What is smile without the /s/?" (*mile*)

Many states are adopting the DIBELS (Dynamic Indicators of Basic Early Literacy Skills) test to assess how children are doing with Reading First and No Child Left Behind initiatives. The DIBELS test is a standardized measure for assessing

- *Phonological awareness:* a child's skill in identifying and producing the initial sounds, and producing the individual sounds, within a given word.
- *Alphabetic principle:* a child's knowledge of letter–sound correspondences, as well as the ability to blend letters together to form unfamiliar "nonsense" words.
- *Fluency with connected text:* a child's skill in reading connected text in grade-level material.

The Dibels test is free to download from the test website at http://dibels.uoregon.edu/

A wide range of informal assessments can be also used to assess fluency, including reading miscue analysis (Goodman and Burke 1972) and running records (Clay 1972; Clay 1993) and informal reading inventories (Johnson, Kress, et al. 1987). Techniques associated with each of these approaches are described in more detail in Chapter 11.

Teaching Reading Fluency

The most important goal in teaching reading fluency is to engage children actively while they build knowledge and skill with oral and written language. Round Robin Reading, a technique that has been used for decades with the intent of developing fluency, is *not* effective (Rasinski and Hoffman 2003). Round Robin Reading, as it is usually practiced, has children reading orally for a teacher who checks for and corrects oral reading errors. Children need specific modeling, coaching, and assistance to improve their oral reading performance. If they read only for themselves, as in Round Robin reading, they do not get the experience of hearing fluent reading or being engaged in ways that are focused on their own particular needs in developing fluency.

Helping children who have only a partial grasp of language involves providing them with many opportunities to hear and experience fluent reading, to build connections between sounds and symbols, and to begin to construct meaning from words (Cunningham 1999). Difficulties with oral language and fluency often stem from inexperience with language and print. For this kind of need, increasing oral language and literacy-building experiences can be a solution. Teaching practices that engage students include (Cunningham 1999; Armbruster, Lehr, et al. 2002)

- Modeling fluent reading for children, having them reread the same texts on their own
- Reading orally with expression and then talking about it
- Practicing probable pronunciations for letters and words—making your "best guess"

- Sorting words according to shape and length
- Connecting, sounds, words, and pictures
- Having students repeatedly read passages aloud with specific guidance
- Asking students to reread text that is reasonably easy for them.
- Practicing oral rereading with partners

Research has shown that it is not the quantity of fluency practice that matters; instead, what matters is how teachers model reading fluency, provide feedback, and help students gain independence in assessing their own fluency (Rasinski and Hoffman 2003). For example, while listening to children's oral reading, teachers should help children build a greater awareness of how they are reading. In the long run, this helps children learn to become more fluent on their own. Futher guidelines for teachers:

- Be selective in what you attend to when giving feedback.
- Ignore miscues that do not change a text's meaning, and wait before responding to miscues that do involve a meaning change.
- Give children the chance to self-monitor and self-correct their performance.
- Offer some "repair" strategies, such as looking at the words around a word and thinking about words that have similar sounds, as clues to the pronunciation and meaning of a word.

There are also ways to incorporate fluency practice within classroom literacy lessons. For example, an Oral Recitation Lesson (ORL) starts with the teacher reading a story to children. This is followed by a discussion that leads to the construction of a story map—a map containing the characters, features of the setting, and major plot events—and a summary of the story. Children then read and reread a section of the story with the teacher, followed by children selecting, practicing, and performing an oral reading of a segment of the story. In addition, children spend a brief period of time practicing stories covered in previous lessons and performing them for the teacher. Sometimes, parents are enlisted in listening to the children read at home (Hoffman and Crone 1985).

Another version of this kind of lesson is the Fluency-Oriented Reading Instruction (FORI) Lesson (Stahl and Heuback in press). Like the ORL, the FORI begins with the teacher reading a passage aloud to the class, followed by a discussion and by vocabulary and comprehension activities. Other instructional activities from the passage are added, including having children reread it with a partner, with the teacher, or independently. Children also reread the passage at home with their parents or another adult over a number of days.

Don't Forget the Needs of Older Students

Practice with oral language and fluency is often omitted for older students, despite the need for many of them to work with ongoing development of these skills. For older students—upper elementary, middle school and high school students—resolve to build in practice with oral language and fluency routinely. Create multiple opportunities for students to communicate with you and each other, as you help them grow in their understanding of standards and in their ability to perform well on required assessments. Worthy and Broaddus (2002) offer the following ideas.

Modeled reading: Teachers read high-interest books aloud to the class, followed by students rereading in groups or individually.

Audiotaped books: Students listen to books read aloud on audiotape, followed by students rereading in groups or individually.

Readers' theater: Have students perform a play by reading it aloud, with expression.

Poetry reading: Divide the class into groups of five, each with responsibility for presenting a poem to the class.

Inspiring speakers: Have students listen to recorded speeches of inspiring speakers (such as Martin Luther King or Maya Angelou). Ask students to read the speeches with their own intonation.

It is important that students, in doing these activities, clearly understand their purposes and roles. Build in ways to engage students specifically in their reading. Oral reading performances should be preceded by a discussion about taking the audience(s) into consideration. Involve students directly in choices of texts for oral reading and in discussions about the kinds of oral expression best suited for particular audiences. Sometimes, older readers can be enlisted to read orally to younger readers. Help the older readers choose simple texts with straightforward plots and simple dialogue. Other audiences could be the elderly or even students themselves. Involving students in choices about audience, text, and expression will help them make connections among fluency, comprehension, and expression.

SPECIAL PROJECTS

For Beginning Teachers

Visit the Dibels website at http://dibels.uoregon.edu/ and download the test. Review the test with respect to

- What it measures
- How it can be used
- How performance on the test predicts students' performance in fluency and other areas of reading

For Experienced Teachers

Review a lesson that you regularly teach. Revise the lesson by including opportunities for practice with fluency and oral language.

SUGGESTED READINGS

Cunningham, P. (1999). *Phonics they use.* Upper Saddle River, NJ: Pearson Education.

Cunningham, P., & Allington, R. (2002). *Classrooms that work: They can all read and write.* New York: Allyn and Bacon.

Pinnell, G., & Fountas, I. (1996). *Guided reading: Good first teaching for all children.* Portsmouth, NH: Heinemann.

Connecting Classroom Practice to Student Achievement

10 Making Sense of Large-scale Assessment Information

How to gather, interpret, and use data from state- and district-level assessments

In this chapter, we will discuss ways of making sense of large-scale information. As school districts and schools face greater pressure to demonstrate annual yearly progress, these kinds of tests are becoming increasingly popular. Knowing how to gather, interpret, and use data from these tests is more important than ever.

Making Sense of Large-scale Tests

In order to interpret data from large-scale tests, it is essential to understand the tests, how and what they measure, and the information they produce. Large-scale tests include state-level competency or proficiency tests, which may or may not be standardized, and such standardized tests as IQ tests, achievement tests, and diagnostic tests. State-level competency or proficiency tests are often not standardized. Standardized tests are frequently used on a large scale—to assess, for example, district- or even state-level reading or mathematics performance. Recall that to be standardized, a test must be submitted to rigorous study, which includes comparing student performance from year to year and comparing one test to an already recognized test. Many state tests are not standardized because of the expense and labor involved in standardizing a test.

Many state tests assess content knowledge: what students know and are able to do in a content area. State tests are often referred to as **criterion-referenced tests;** students need to perform at a specified level (criterion) in order to be judged proficient or competent in a subject matter domain. For many of these tests, a cutoff score is selected using a variety of criteria. Students who score above the cutoff score "pass," or are deemed proficient, and students who score below it are labeled "less than proficient," "emerging," or "failing." A controversy with these tests is how the cutoff score should be derived: by using statistics (for example, everyone above the average passes) or simply by picking a number.

There are many different types of standardized tests, including tests that measure achievement (Figure 10.1), those that measure intelligence (Figure 10.2), and those that diagnose problems that students may have in their learning (Figure 10.3).

FIGURE 10.1   **Standardized Achievement Tests**

California Achievement Tests — Reading—Grades K through 9. CTB/McGraw-Hill.

Comprehensive Tests of Basic Skills (Spanish edition available)—Grades K through 9. CTB/McGraw-Hill.

Educational Development Series—1984 Edition (EDS)—Grades K through 12. Riverside Publishing Company.

Gates–MacGinitie Reading Test, revised edition—Grades 1 through 12. Riverside Publishing Company.

Iowa Silent Reading Test (ISRT)—Grades 6 through college. Psychological Corporation.

Iowa Test of Basic Skills (ITBS)—Grades 6 through college. Psychological Corporation.

Metropolitan Achievement Test—Grades K through 12. Psychological Corporation.

Nelson–Denny Reading Test—Grades 9 through 12. Riverside Publishing Company.

Nelson–Denny Reading Skills Test—Grades 3 through 9. Riverside Publishing Company.

SRA Achievement Series—Grades K through 12. Science Research Associates.

Stanford Achievement Test—Grades 1 through 9. Psychological Corporation.

Stanford Test of Academic Skills—Grades 8 through college freshman. Psychological Corporation.

Tests of Achievement and Proficiency—Grades 9 through 12. Riverside Publishing Company.

FIGURE 10.2   **Some Commonly Used Intelligence (IQ) Tests**

Kaufman Assessment Battery for Children—Ages 2.5 through 12.5. American Guidance Service.

Peabody Picture Vocabulary Test—Ages 2 through 18. American Guidance Service.

Slosson Intelligence Test for Children and Adults (SIT)—Infants and older. Slosson Educational Publications.

Stanford–Binet Intelligence Scale, fourth edition (S-B)—Ages 2 and up. Riverside Publishing Company.

Wechsler Intelligence Scale for Children (WISC-R)—Ages 6 through 16. Psychological Corporation.

IQ tests are used as an indicator of an individual's potential for learning. A standardized **achievement test** is "an assessment that measures a student's *acquired knowledge and skills* in one or more common content areas (McGraw-Hill 2003).

Diagnostic tests are given usually as a follow-up to IQ and achievement tests. **Diagnostic tests** are "intended to *locate learning difficulties* or patterns of error." (McGraw-Hill 2003). These tests often reveal specific areas of need with respect to reading and mathematics. On the basis of the results of diagnostic tests, students are placed in special educational programs and are provided specific kinds of instruction tailored to their needs.

FIGURE 10.3   Some Commonly Used Diagnostic Reading Tests

Diagnostic Achievement Battery (DAB)—Ages 6 through 14. Pro-Ed.

Diagnostic Reading Scales, revised edition—First through seventh grade reading levels. CTB/McGraw-Hill.

Doren Diagnostic Reading Test of Word Recognition Skills—Grades 1 through 6. American Guidance Service.

Durrell Analysis of Reading Difficulty, revised edition—first through sixth grade reading levels. American Guidance Service.

Gates–McKillop–Horowitz Reading Diagnostic Test—Used at the first through sixth grade reading levels. Teachers College Press.

MsCullough Word-Analysis Test—Intermediate grades (5 through 8). Chapman, Brook & Kent.

Sipay Word Analysis Test (SWAT)—Elementary school. Educators Publishing Service.

Stanford Diagnostic Reading Test—Grades K through college freshman. Harcourt Assessment.

Wide-Range Achievement Tests WRAT—Ages 5 through adult. Stoelting Company.

Woodcock Reading Mastery Test—Grades K through 12. American Guidance Service.

Lately, standardized tests have become popular in assessing early literacy performance. Other early literacy tests measure these same variables but also assess vocabulary knowledge, comprehension, and writing. Tests like these are used for a number of purposes, from determining which students require early intervention to demonstrating achievement at the individual, classroom, and district levels.

Many school districts these days are adopting standardized tests at every grade level because of new federal mandates, such as No Child Left Behind and Reading First, for early intervention and accountability for annual yearly progress at every grade level. In many cases, educators are opting for standardized tests because of their ease of administration and scoring, convenient reporting based on rigorous study of validity and reliability, and lower cost compared with state tests. On the other hand, standardized tests are often not as detailed with respect to content area concepts and expectations, and therefore, they may not be consistent with existing standards and assessments. For example, a standardized test might offer general tasks and scores for word recognition when early elementary teachers need information about phonological awareness, or a comprehension score might be derived from a standardized test when teachers are interested in a measure of social studies or science knowledge or skill.

Making Sense of Large-scale Test Scores

One of the challenges in making sense of large-scale tests is making sense of the scores they yield. Figure 10.4 lists some of the terms used in reporting students' performance. Raw scores are almost never emphasized on large-scale tests. A

FIGURE 10.4   **Some Ways of Reporting Data from Large-Scale Tests**

Raw score: The number of correct answers. This is the basis for all other scores.

Grade equivalent: These scores place students on the continuum of grade levels and months within grade levels. For instance, a student might achieve a score of 4.1. This translates into a score of Fourth Grade, First Month. This may not be a concern if the student is a fourth grader in the early part of the year, but it can be a concern if the student is a sixth or even eighth grader.

Percentile rank: Tells what percentage of students in the norm group the student outscored. The norm group is the group of students used to develop the test. This is the group that is always used in comparisons with the test taker's performance. A student with a percentile rank of 85 outscored 85 percent of the students in the norm group who took the test before.

Scaled score: Raw scores are converted into a single scale with intervals of equal size.

Stanine: Raw scores are converted so that students' scores are placed on a scale of 1 through 9. Scores in the upper third are said to be superior. Those in the lower third are below average. Students who score in the mid-range, 4 through 6, are said to be average.

reason for this is that most, if not all, large-scale tests are concerned with comparing an individual's performance to the performance of individuals within a large group. If a student receives a score of 6 correct items out of 10, it says nothing about how the student performed with respect to the larger group. It is more likely that the score will be converted—to a grade equivalent, a percentile, a stanine, or some other scale—so that the student's performance can be interpreted relative to a group's performance. As a result, the student scoring "6" might actually be performing on a par with other students in fourth grade (a grade equivalent), or in the 50th percentile (in the middle of all students taking the test), or in the 8th stanine (in the upper levels of achievement).

Many state-level tests convert students' raw scores to another scale, using a mathematical formula. This is sometimes done by multiplying each raw score by some factor or formula. The result is usually a spreading out of the data. Thus, if a test has 20 items, each score might be multiplied by 30, so that the scores range from 30 to 600. The possible scores are separated by 30 points, rather than 1. Why would test makers decide to do this? The argument goes that tests can vary in difficulty, and scaling is a way to control for changes in performance due to differences in difficulty. In practice, this means that a state can examine test performance each year and establish a different cutoff score for passing and failing each year (Popham 2003). Hence, rather than saying that getting 7 out of 20 items (or 65 percent) correct means failure every year, a state can convert the scores to a broader scale and set failure rates each year, according to the overall test performance.

For instance, setting a standard failure rate of 65 percent each year could lead to a fluctuating percentage of students passing—due largely to differences in the tests—from 30 percent of the students passing one year to 70 percent passing another year. Resetting the cutoff point each year, according to the overall performance on the test, through scaling, can lead to a consistent rate of percentages of students passing and failing: 50 percent passing, 65 percent passing, and so on.

Of course, as you know if you've followed the argument for scaling so far, this also means that the scaling of state tests can open the door to all sorts of interpretation and manipulation. Through scaling, state officials can set a cutoff point that is politically advantageous or that reflects badly on some schools and/or programs. That's why it is vital to study student performance very carefully over periods of time and in comparison with other indicators of performance. The following sections demonstrate how to do this.

Look at Data from at Least Three Years

The newspapers do it all the time, with headlines such as "Smallville outperforms Dogpatch once again!" and "Park Place does well for third year in a row!" These comparisons generate lots of public pressure from school boards, parents, and the business community. Although it is not necessarily a bad thing for the public to be involved in what happens in schools, there is considerable room for misinterpretation of test results through the comparisons often made in the media. A good example is the media practice of showing only two-year patterns or results when reporting test scores. Schools and educators need to be proactive in organizing and presenting responsible comparisons that give a more comprehensive picture of how students and schools are doing. The first step is ensuring that public scrutiny of test results is concentrated on patterns of performance that extend out at least three years.

Consider the pattern of results depicted in Figure 10.5 for reading performance in the fourth grade for a single year, 2002. Troy Elementary and East Grand Rapids Elementary shine in relation to the other schools, and it is not surprising: These schools are in communities where most of the families are in a higher socioeconomic bracket, compared with the other schools. Charter Elementary, an urban charter school, demonstrates the least successful performance, with the largest proportion of low-performing students.

Typically, the media take patterns like this and form conclusions, such as "Public schools outperform charter schools." Politicians or teacher unions may run with this, concluding that charter schools are a failed experiment. But before we drive the final nail into the coffin of charter schools, we need more information.

Consider Figures 10.6 and 10.7, which depict student performance over a four-year period. Several additional observations can be made on the basis of these figures. Though Charter Elementary was outperformed by all of the other schools, it did manage to maintain the small proportion of successfully performing students. The proportion of successfully performing students did not go down over the four years. On the other hand, the numbers of low-performing students went up dramatically. What could account for these patterns?

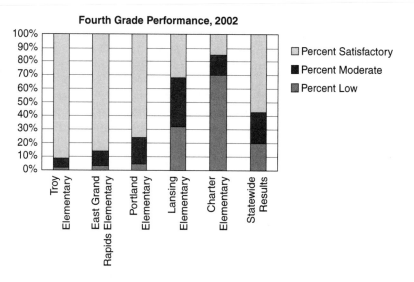

FIGURE 10.5   Reading Performance For a Single Year, Michigan Educational Assessment Program Test

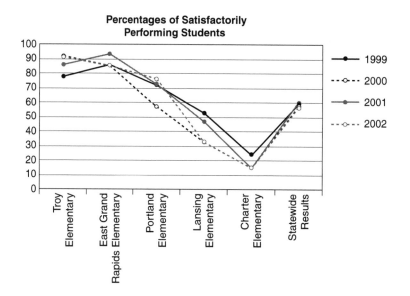

FIGURE 10.6   Reading Performance for Multiple Years, Michigan Educational Assessment Program Test

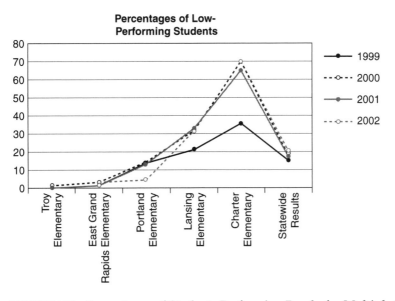

FIGURE 10.7 Percentages of Students Performing Poorly for Multiple Years, Michigan Educational Assessment Program Test

To understand the full story, one needs to understand the history of Charter Elementary. Charter Elementary began as a charter school dedicated to serving special education students through the use of technology. In the early years, the school managed to attract a mix of both special education and regular education students from city school districts. Then, as the school became known for its successful work with special education students, more and more special education students flocked to the school. The downside of this trend was a precipitous slide in test scores. This school works very hard on alternative assessments so that it can demonstrate growth in learning, despite what the state tests report. A constant challenge for the school is to get out its message that despite the state test scores, students are learning. Proud of their success, educators in this school develop alternative assessments and devise their own communications about these assessments, rather than changing their mission of dedication to students who struggle.

Portland Elementary presents a slightly different picture. In most years, Portland, a rural school, demonstrates a pattern of performance that is consistent with the state average, for both low-performing and successfully performing students. In the year 2000, the proportion of successfully performing students dropped, and there were no comparable changes in the state or in other districts. This pattern could be caused by many factors, such as an influx of students into the school or district, a significant curriculum change, or staff reassignments or retirements.

Similarly, the proportion of low-performing students *dropped* in the year 2002, a year when most other schools either stayed the same or increased slightly in low-performing students. Again, the causes for this drop in least successful students could be many: a new, effective curriculum, staff development, and/or other changes in the ways that teachers work with students.

Far too often, the media overlook these complex patterns and their causes in favor of easy targets: The schools did or didn't do their job, the teachers are bad (or good), and schools and/or teachers in one school or district are good (or bad). It is our responsibility as educators to help parents and others see the whole picture. It is clear from these examples that numbers, particularly numbers from a single year of test performance, do not tell the whole tale. Chapter 12 details some strategies for communicating a more complete picture.

Make Appropriate Comparisons between How You Did and How Everyone Else Did

As these illustrations depict, different communities naturally and consistently perform differently, particularly with large-scale assessments. The reasons for this may be obvious: socioeconomic status, educational opportunities, or even values placed on education and, more specifically, on literacy.

Some comparisons are blatantly unfair. For example, comparing a high-socioeconomic-status community such East Grand Rapids with a lower-SES community such as Lansing is inappropriate. Children in Lansing simply do not have the same access to enriching experiences as children in higher-SES communities. These experiences include access to libraries, books, motivating print, educational vacations, and the Internet. Many students arrive in large urban schools each day hungry and stressed out, something their suburban counterpart are much less likely to experience. Although it has become popular in some political circles to say that children just need to work harder, comparing the test performances of children across widely disparate schools and communities often overlooks a very uneven playing field.

What, then, constitutes fair comparisons? The answer lies in comparing comparable communities as well as comparing student performance within a school to student performance within a larger state or region. Note the similarities in performance between East Grand Rapids and Troy Elementary. This is logical, given that the communities are similar in demographics. Were test performance to go up or down in comparison with one another in a given year, there would be reason for concern or celebration. With community characteristics held constant, each school can draw conclusions about patterns of performance that are more valid than those based on comparisons with a rural, middle-class school such as Portland or with an urban school district characterized by some poverty, such as Lansing.

The other useful comparison is to the state averages and trends. If the scores of a school or district rise in a year when the state scores go down, there is cause for celebration of success. On the other hand, a school's scores going down while the state scores hold steady or even rise should occasion much soul-searching and research into why the scores went down. Consequently, strive for comparisons—and help others make comparisons that are appropriate—by comparing comparable schools and communities and by studying trends in the larger state or region over time.

What Item Analyses Can (and What They Cannot) Do for You

Many schools and districts engage in many different forms of item analysis as a way to target instruction toward improving test performance. A popular way to do this is to take a careful look at the students who are very close to—but not quite—passing. The rationale for this is simple, if troubling. In a sort of triage approach, schools do not concentrate on the higher-performing students because their scores will not rise a great deal with extra instruction. Similarly, students at the lowest levels of performance often lack the skills or the will necessary to make considerable gains on tests. Students in the middle, by comparison, may be motivated to do better and may have missed only a few items that might be easily remediated, thereby boosting the school's overall test performance.

Intermediate school districts, Boards of Cooperative Educational Services (BOCES), and school district central offices commonly have test analysis specialists who can disaggregate data, depicting patterns of performance for individual items. Careful analysis of student performance on individual tests items is referred to as **item analysis.** Consider this example.

Decatur School District and Sunnyside School District both have 50 percent of their students passing a state reading test, and both want to improve. However, the patterns of performance in the districts are quite different (Figure 10.8). Decatur has a substantial number of students in the bottom quarter, compared with Sunnyside, a district with considerable numbers of students in the third quarter.

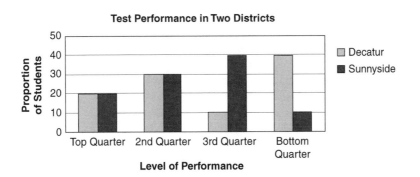

FIGURE 10.8   Test Performance in Two Districts

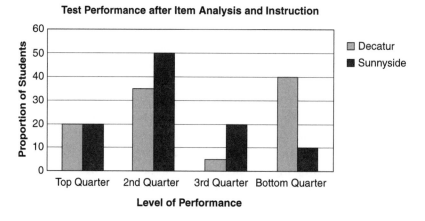

FIGURE 10.9   Test Performance After Item Analysis and Instruction

To improve, both districts analyzed the performance data and discovered that students in the third level of performance missed a lot of questions involving themes for narrative stories. Students in the fourth level of performance, by comparison, missed many different types of items, too many different types for a pattern to emerge. As a result, both districts emphasized the teaching and learning of narrative themes, particularly in English and reading classes for average students, in an attempt to boost the scores. What happened?

Figure 10.9 depicts a hypothetical set of results for our scenario. One key number has changed: Sunnyside managed to move many more students from the third quarter into the second quarter, increasing the overall proportion of successful students from 50 percent to 70 percent. In comparison, Decatur managed to move only 5 percent of its students above the 50 percent point, for an overall success rate of 55 percent. Consider what often happens in the media under these circumstances: Sunnyside is championed as an improving school district, while Decatur is ignored or even criticized for such modest improvement.

One could argue that these conclusions are unfair for many reasons. First, Sunnyside had a much easier task, with far more students who might respond positively to targeted instruction in the third quarter. Decatur, on the other hand, had many more students, with many more needs, struggling to succeed at the bottom levels of performance.

Again, the learning challenges—and the communication challenges—under these circumstances are extremely important. It may be possible for some schools and districts to do targeted instruction based on item analysis and produce improvement for a certain segment of students, but many other schools and districts face complex patterns of performance, especially among those students who are the hardest to reach and teach. It is still necessary to understand and respond to the true nature of the challenges faced, given distinct patterns of student performance. Item analysis is just one useful tool.

Separate Content Knowledge from Test-Taking Ability

Yet another issue in making sense of test performance is the need to separate content knowledge from test-taking ability. Many schools and districts spend considerable amounts of time reorganizing curricula so that students learn content necessary for passing tests at appropriate times. An excellent example of this kind of reorganization concerns the appearance of questions involving statistics for students in very early grades, whereas before, statistics had been taught only at the high school if not college levels. When statistics began to be emphasized on early second or third grade tests, in the form of organizing data or thinking about organized data, publishers and curriculum developers followed with materials to help students learn about statistics. A comparable change has taken place within science and social studies curricula, which have been restructured to emphasize more personal involvement with inquiry around both subjects. Similarly, there is greater concern for informational materials for very young children within reading and language arts.

Although some poor test performance can be blamed on failure to change curriculum content in keeping with changes in tests, some of the blame also goes to students' unfamiliarity with tests, particularly with ways in which questions are asked about new content. Numerous schools and districts report making valiant efforts at restructuring curricula with respect to tests, only to see their students perform poorly because little, if any, preparation was done to help students use their new content knowledge with the formats and item types that appeared on the tests.

The solution to this dilemma is quite simple. Take some time—and not even a lot of time—to familiarize students with assessment in relation to the new content. After students have learned something new, ask them to write some questions that they or a teacher might ask on a test of the content. Discuss what makes a good test question about the content and what makes a bad question. Also talk about good answers to different questions. This can be a way to strike an appropriate balance between the need to help students understand important content and the need to familiarize students with assessment surrounding what they have learned.

Refocus Teaching and Learning on the Basis of What You Learn from Tests

As the previous sections have demonstrated, the job of refocusing teaching and learning on the basis of test performance is both complex and important. Resist the urge to look for easy answers. As the previous examples illustrate, what seem to be obvious patterns of performance may actually be misconceptions that lead to an overemphasis on some students and skills or to the neglect of students who struggle the most or of skills that students genuinely need. Effective focusing of the curriculum to enhance test performance comes from looking beneath the obvious patterns, making relevant comparisons, and then setting and acting on appropriate goals for teaching and learning.

SPECIAL PROJECTS

For Beginning Teachers

Test results for schools are usually reported in local newspapers and on state Department of Education websites. Locate the test scores for the schools in your area. How many years of scores are usually reported? Compare the scores for different school districts. What conclusions can you draw about the test performance of different school districts in your area?

For Experienced Teachers

With some colleagues, gather the test performance data for your school over the past three or more years. Include data from a comparable school and from the state or region in which you live. Draw some conclusions about how your school is doing. What factors could be responsible for the trends?

SUGGESTED READINGS

Calkins, L., Montgomery, K., & Santman, D. (1998). *A teacher's guide to standardized reading tests: Knowledge is power.* Portsmouth, NH: Heinemann.
Popham, W. J. (2003). *Test better, teach better: The instructional role of assessment.* Alexandria, VA: ASCD.

CHAPTER

11

Selecting, Designing, and Using Classroom Assessments

How to design, implement, and interpret tests that are made especially for classroom use, keeping standards and high-stakes assessment in mind

I learned my favorite metaphor for everyday learning in schools from an art teacher friend of mine: "It's like a long-running movie, changing every day." Classroom assessments—observations, talking with students, informal assessments, content area inventories, tests, quizzes, projects, classroom work—are all part of the movie. Classroom assessments document growth in students over time. In contrast, large-scale tests, such as those discussed in previous chapters, are like snapshots; they focus on achievement at key moments.

Good assessment incorporates a concern for both—the movie that plays every day, showing students being challenged and growing in their learning *and* the snapshots that depict the plateaus and valleys of achievement. Without the sense of day-to-day growth in students that classroom assessments provide, it is difficult to understand their long-term achievement or help them with it. Worse yet, without a sense of their day-to-day learning, we get very little indication of when students falter or are in trouble or of what we can do to help them. At the same time, although it is not exactly popular to champion achievement tests, few would argue that we need some indication of what students have learned at different points in time. Some argue in favor of large-scale tests as a way to tell when schools themselves are in trouble and need help. But it can remain unclear what kinds of help are needed until we know a great deal more about what happens with learning in classrooms every day. That's where classroom assessment plays an important role.

Classroom assessment should be purposeful, rich, and varied. We want to develop an ongoing picture of our students' developing content knowledge, their skills, and their dispositions—attitudes and feelings about literacy and the content they are learning. Using many assessment tools helps us make better decisions about the help students need. Multiple and varied assessments also provide new and different opportunities for students to revisit, rethink, and internalize what they are learning. Don't forget to consider carefully how existing standards and high-stakes tests are related to your own goals in classroom assessment.

FIGURE 11.1   Kidwatching—Observing Students Reading

Before reading, the strategic reader:

Analyzes reading tasks and goals (What am I being asked to read or do with the reading?)

Previews texts

Activates prior knowledge

Sets purpose(s) for reading

During reading, the strategic reader:

Predicts content, events, and outcomes

Raises questions about texts

Looks for important ideas and relationships

Makes inferences

Monitors comprehension (Am I making sense of things?)

Uses fix-up strategies when comprehension isn't working (Reads ahead for clarification, rereads, uses other strategies as required, cross-checks for unknown words)

Integrates new information with prior knowledge

Responds personally to text

After reading, the strategic reader:

Reconstructs concepts, events, and/or relationships

Summarizes and/or paraphrases text

Reflects on text, relating it to purpose(s) for reading

The following sections detail a number of classroom assessment tools that you may find useful. We'll start with assessments that are designed for determining how a child sees himself or herself as a reader. Then we will look at measures of fluency and comprehension, assessments of content area literacy, and, finally, portfolios. The chapter concludes with some simple guidelines for interpreting and refocusing classroom assessment on the basis of students' performance.

Kidwatching

Kidwatching is a term used to describe the process of observing students as they read and write (Goodman 2002). Kidwatching can take place in all sorts of teaching and learning contexts. Through kidwatching, teachers can gain useful insight into a child's reading and writing performance and developing knowledge. Classroom observations of students are often one of the most undervalued areas of assessment, but experienced teachers know how important regular kidwatching can be for observing the growth and the challenges their students experience.

To make the most of kidwatching, it is important to reflect on the learning goals you have in mind. Figures 11.1 and 11.2 depict observation checklists (Leslie and Jett-Simpson 1997) that you may wish to consider using while observing students read and write. Other kinds of checklist are possible—for instance, checklists designed for observing students in their content area classes. Kidwatching is a relatively easy way to observe how students are growing in their understandings.

FIGURE 11.2   Kidwatching—Observing Students Writing

Are students doing any prewriting, such as:

    brainstorming?

    talking to others or observing others?

    thinking to themselves?

    drawing or visualizing?

    free writing?

    organizing ideas (note taking, webbing, mapping)?

During drafting, are students:

    focusing on an idea or set of ideas?

    refocusing ideas when they get off track?

    revisiting idea generation strategies such as those used in prewriting?

    ignoring mechanics (spelling, punctuation, grammar)?

When students revise, do they:

    reread silently and aloud to themselves?

    self-check, asking "Does this make sense?" "Can I use better words?" "Did I include enough for the reader to understand me?"

    confer with others for feedback?

    use feedback to rearrange text, revise language, and add to or subtract from text?

When students edit, do they:

    reread and apply self-correction strategies for mechanics (spelling, punctuation, grammar)?

    self-check and self-correct, using an editing checklist or other print source such as the dictionary, computer spell check, print around the classroom or language arts text?

    confer with others?

Interviews and Conversations

Interviews and conversations—with students, their parents, and teacher colleagues—can yield extremely valuable information about how a child feels about her or his own literacy, how he or she learns, and how you can help. Interviews and conversations can offer multiple lenses through which to view students' literacy abilities. There are different kinds of questions you may wish to consider for interviews and conversations with your students, with their parents, and with other teachers who may be able to offer insight about how your students learn.

Good readers and writers not only comprehend and compose well but also know how they do it and what to do when it is not working for them. The opposite is often true for struggling readers and writers: They do not know when they are in trouble, and when they *are* having difficulty, they do not know how to help themselves. The following questions will help you learn how much students know about themselves as readers and writers. Sometimes, it is helpful to have a student bring a favorite book or a recent writing sample when asking these questions (Leslie and Jett-Simpson 1997).

- Are you a good reader/writer? Why or why not?
- Do you know anyone who is a good reader/writer?
- What does this person do that makes her or him a good reader/writer?
- When you are reading, what do you do when you come to something you do not know?
- What is your favorite book? Why?

Ask these questions about recent writing that the student has completed:

- What kind of writing is this?
- What did you have to do or think about to write this?
- Is this writing finished? How do you know when your writing is finished?
- What kinds of writing do you do in school?
- Do you do any writing outside of school? What kinds?

The purpose of interviewing parents is to gain some insight into a child's literate activities at home. Parents see their children in many different settings, using reading and writing in ways that are different from their use in school.

- Tell me about your child, including what it has been like for him or her to grow up, likes, and dislikes.
- What kinds of reading or writing do you do at home?
- Does your child talk about any favorite subjects in school? What does your child like about them?
- What kinds of reading have you observed your child doing at home?
- Does your child enjoy reading (or writing)? Why or why not?

- What are your child's favorite books or stories?
- What kinds of television does your child enjoy watching?
- Does your child spend any time on the Internet? If so, what kinds of Internet sites does your child enjoy?

Teachers who have had your student before can provide insight into how she or he has developed as a reader or writer. Of course, some students are so young that they may have had little contact with other teachers. That can be an important detail too. The following questions can help you learn what other teachers have observed about your student's reading and writing.

- Is (child's name) a good reader? Is (child's name) a good writer? How do you know?
- What kinds of reading and writing have you observed (child's name) doing?
- Are there any areas where (child's name) excels in reading and writing?
- Are there any areas where (child's name) has experienced difficulty in reading and writing?

Reading Miscue Inventories

A **reading miscue inventory** (or **miscue analysis**) is an assessment technique used to analyze the patterns of oral reading performance that a reader demonstrates (Goodman 1969). A **miscue** is the difference between what a text says and how a reader reads the text orally. Miscue analysis starts with a child reading a text orally, usually followed by the reader retelling or summarizing what has been read. Comparisons are then made between the oral reading performance and the retellings to observe relationships between fluency and comprehension (Goodman and Burke 1972).

Texts offer up different kinds of cues for a reader to follow during oral reading: the letters (graphic information); the order of words—termed **syntax**—that indicates their grammatical function; and the meanings of words—termed **semantics.** Readers are required to supply their own knowledge, connecting their understandings of spoken language to written symbols, their knowledge of grammatical function, and their understanding of meanings of words. The purpose of miscue analysis is to study a reader's miscues—differences between oral readings and what the text says—for signs of how the reader uses text cues and for signs of understandings of language and how language works.

Proficient or good readers are able to use all available text cues and their understandings of language to construct meaning. In fact, good readers rely strategically on some cues more than others, depending on the situations they encounter, such as unfamiliar vocabulary and their own inexperience with certain phrases. For example, good readers often construct an overall sense of the gist of what they are reading and thus make continual, accurate predictions about their reading.

Sometimes their predictions are inaccurate—for instance, saying *cheddar* for *cheese*—but do not drastically interfere with their sense making. In fact, as in this example, their predictions preserve the meaning.

In contrast, less proficient or struggling readers do not know exactly what to do when they encounter something they don't know in print. They may rely haphazardly on letters, sounds, and/or words without constructing meaning appropriately. Sometimes, struggling readers over-rely on cues in print—laboriously pronouncing letters, saying one word at a time without making connections—at the expense of garnering any meaning. They may have little, if any, awareness of how they are reading and whether they are being successful (Goodman 1999). A reading miscue inventory can be a way to tell who is struggling and why and how to go about helping them.

To understand more about miscues, consider these examples. Suppose a reader encounters a word, such as *baby*, but reads it any of the following ways:

- baby
- ba-ba-
- bear
- ear
- skipping the word altogether

These patterns reflect different understandings of the word, as the reader attends to or does not attend to different kinds of language cues, such as letters and the beginning, middle, or ending of the word.

Miscues are always considered in the context in which they appear—sentences, phrases, and longer passages that give individual words both grammatical function and meaning. Consider for example, the following pattern for one reader:

Child Reading	The plane flew higher as it headed for Alabama.
Text	The airplane sailed high as it headed for Atlanta.

Note that in this example, some of the words change the meaning (saying *Alabama* instead of *Atlanta*), whereas others do not (saying *plane* for *airplane*, and saying *flew* for *sailed*). From this small piece of information, one could conclude that this is a reader who has some basic understandings about language but may be lacking in others. A reading miscue inventory represents a systematic approach to understanding a child's knowledge and beliefs about how language works while reading orally (Goodman and Burke 1972).

There are many different kinds of miscues:

- In **substitutions,** the reader substitutes a different word for a word in the text.
- In **insertions,** the reader inserts a word that does not appear in the text.
- In **omissions,** the reader omits (does not say) a word that is in the text.

- In **partials,** the reader says only a part of a word, such as a beginning, a middle, or an ending.
- In **self-corrections,** the reader performs a miscue but corrects it.

Preparing for a reading miscue inventory involves selecting, or having the child select, a text for oral reading. If you select the text for the child, select one that appears to be challenging but not too difficult for the child. Having children select the text themselves offers the advantage of revealing their reading choices. A child with limited knowledge of reading, including poor fluency, might select a text that is much too difficult. Other choices will reveal a lot about a child's preferred genres, topics of interest, and favorite authors. Observe during the reading how body language and expression can offer clues to a child's attitudes about reading. To prepare, some teachers make a copy of the text selection to facilitate marking a reader's miscues in the space above each word in the text. Some teachers prefer to audio-record a child's reading so that the reading can be reviewed over and over again, sometimes with the child, to gain a better understanding of his or her miscue patterns.

FIGURE 11.3   Documenting a Child's Oral Reading Performance

Text	Reader	Substitution	Insertion	Omission	Partial	Self-correction	Grammatical Change	Meaning Change	Graphic Similarity		
									High	Medium	Low

Teachers often use a checklist, such as the one depicted in Figure 11.3, to document a child's oral reading performance. Note that this chart contains all of the possible miscues, along with several new categories: grammatical change, meaning change, and a judgment about graphic similarity. **Grammatical change** refers to whether or not the miscue involves a change in grammar, such as inserting an adjective where a noun is supposed to go:

Child Reading   The busy fell out of his chair.
Text   The boy fell out of his chair.

Meaning change refers to whether or not the miscue involves a change in meaning, as in this example:

Child Reading   That small bar is too tall for me.
Text   That small car is too small for me.

Finally, **graphic similarity** refers to whether or not the miscue bears any resemblance to the appearance of a word in the text. For instance:

Child Reading   That boy fell out on his bottom.
Text   The boy flipped out of his chair.

FIGURE 11.4   **One Reader's Pattern of Miscues**

Text	Reader	Substitution	Insertion	Omission	Partial	Self-correction	Grammatical Change	Meaning Change	Graphic Similarity		
									High	Medium	Low
The	that	X								X	
green	gr-				X			X		X	
truck	train	X						X		X	
ran	ran								X		
through	throw	X					X			X	
the	the								X		
—	red							X			
stop	—			X							
sign	s- s- sign					X			X		

Note that some of the words read by this child bear a high resemblance (*that* for *the*), some a medium resemblance (*fell* for *flipped*), and some little or low resemblance (*bottom* for *chair*) to the word in the text. Each of these examples illustrates the different ways that a reader can attend to different aspects of text information.

To see how the process of marking miscues works, study the chart that has been filled out in Figure 11.4 on the basis of one child's reading performance. Note that this child often substitutes other words for words in the text and that his miscues sometimes involve a change in meaning. In retelling the sentence, this child corrected himself, acknowledging that the sentence really was about a *truck* rather than a *train*. From this brief segment, one could conclude that this is a reader who sees the first part of a word and then rushes on to say the rest of the word without thinking about it.

Miscue analysis is not complete until miscue patterns are compared with how a child comprehends what she or he has read. To assess comprehension, teachers ask children to retell what they have read, saying, "Tell me everything you know about what you have just read." Sometimes teachers ask questions about what a child says during a retelling, following the rule that questions should at first be derived only from what the child includes in the retelling. A scoring guide such as the one shown in Figure 11.5 is used to develop a rough measure of how much the child comprehends from the reading.

Once the reader's pattern of miscues is identified and comprehension has been assessed, it becomes possible to consider what he or she needs to improve.

FIGURE 11.5 A Guide for Scoring a Reader's Retelling/Summary

Informational Text	No		Partial		Yes
Major concepts	1	2	3	4	5
Generalizations	1	2	3	4	5
Specific details	1	2	3	4	5
Organization	1	2	3	4	5
Overall retelling	1	2	3	4	5
Narrative Text	**No**		**Partial**		**Yes**
Character recall	1	2	3	4	5
Character development	1	2	3	4	5
Setting	1	2	3	4	5
Relationship of events	1	2	3	4	5
Plot	1	2	3	4	5
Theme	1	2	3	4	5
Overall retelling	1	2	3	4	5

FIGURE 11.6   Some Common Miscue Patterns and Strategies for Helping Students

Some Common Miscue Patterns	Related Teaching and Learning Strategies
Lots of partials and omissions as the child attempts to pronounce words but recognizes only the beginnings and endings of words. May be little graphic similarity between miscues and text. Very little understanding evident from a recall.	Possible problems with phonemic awareness and phonological awareness. Require basic work with fluency (see Chapter 9), teaching spoken sounds and sound–symbol relationships.
High frequency of miscues that change the meaning; few attempts at self-correction. Recall shows very little understanding of the text.	Problems with fluency and comprehension. Analyze miscues for frequent patterns. Provide help with fluency and sense making.
Low frequency of miscues, but slow or labored reading. High graphic similarity when miscues occur. Good understanding demonstrated through recall.	If given enough time, this reader can comprehend. Provide more experience with print, through pleasure reading. Offer help in using context to make sense of the big picture while reading.
High frequency of miscues, uncorrected, but with little meaning change. Excellent recall.	This pattern is often found with older, more experienced readers. They pay attention to the meaning but gloss over the printed words.
High graphic similarity between miscues and text, but little understanding exhibited in the recall.	The reader is paying so much attention to the text that meaning is being sacrificed. Needs more experience with print, especially through pleasure reading. Practice sense making by stopping periodically while asking *What does this say?* and *What does this mean?*

Some children need help with basic fluency, others with comprehension. Some common miscue patterns and some ways of helping students with their oral reading, are given in Figure 11.6.

More recently, miscue analysis has recognized the importance of readers' beliefs about themselves as well as their strategic knowledge about reading (Goodman 1999). **Retrospective miscue analysis** involves having students listen to tape recordings of their own reading so that they can develop better awareness of how they read. Teachers preselect miscues that children have made and point them out while the students are listening to themselves read. Next, they discuss patterns of miscues, including text clues that led a child to make particular kinds of miscues. After some modeling and practice, children are encouraged to select their own miscues for discussion. The intent of this process is to help students discover and develop better self-awareness and control over how they deal with print—as well as to help teachers better understand students' level of strategic awareness of language and print. Teachers who discover, for example, that children are aware of few options when they come to something they do not know, can use retrospective miscue analysis to help them build a stronger repertoire of strategies for reading text and extracting its meaning.

Running Records

Making a **running record** involves taking notes that document a child's oral reading performance while a child reads (Clay 1993). In contrast to miscue analysis, which is often used in one-on-one situations, running records are useful during individual and whole-class reading. Running records can be completed "on the fly" with a minimum of preparation. All that is required is a knowledge of miscues (see the last section) and a chart to document the patterns of miscues.

Figure 11.7 offers one example of a chart that can be used for running records (from (Leslie and Jett-Simpson 1997). On the left is the text the child is reading. On the right is the chart where the teacher has documented the child's oral reading performance, using a check mark whenever the child reads text accurately and recording the number of attempts and the word the child says when the child performs a miscue. The analysis of running records can proceed in the same way as miscue analysis. Watch for how children

- use letters and words to construct meaning
- use strategies to figure out language when they come to something they do not know
- self-correct and monitor their oral reading and comprehension
- use predictions to figure out what they are reading
- demonstrate fluency
- talk about text after reading

Making running records regularly during whole-class oral reading can offer insights into common patterns that children exhibit in oral reading and in their understandings about language. Analyzing running records can help teachers make decisions about instruction, focusing, for example, on different aspects of fluency and comprehension, depending on where children are in their reading development.

Informal Reading Inventories

The purpose of an **informal reading inventory** (IRI) is to gather information about a child's reading fluency and comprehension (Paris and Carpenter 2003). Although there are a great number of informal reading inventories available from commercial publishers (see Figure 11.8), many state education departments across the United States are also producing them, usually in conjunction with high-stakes state tests.

IRIs usually contain oral reading assessments such as miscue analysis (Goodman and Burke 1972) or running records (Clay 1993). Many include graded word lists and reading passages, from preprimer/preschool through middle and high school levels. As children read the word lists and reading passages, teachers record their reading behaviors and ask questions about their understandings. Next, teachers analyze children's reading performance, looking for patterns. The strength of an informal reading inventory is that it focuses on the development of early reading skills, regardless of the age of the learner. As a result, an IRI is useful for early prevention of reading failure in young children (Snow, Burns, et al. 1998), for identification of struggling readers so that they can get the right kinds of help (Alvermann 2001), and for diagnostic assessment of English as a Second Language and adult literacy learners (Paris and Carpenter 2003).

Informal reading inventories are extremely flexible and can be given somewhat frequently. Some teachers use them to assess reading performance at the beginning, middle, and end of the school year. Used at the beginning of the year, an IRI can help with placement and grouping decisions and with decisions about what to teach and to whom. IRIs administered later in the year can provide a picture of how students are developing.

Each IRI is a little different and it is important to select one according to your assessment purposes. If assessing reading fluency is your goal, choose an IRI that

FIGURE 11.7   Making a Running Record

Name_____ Date _____		
Text Title _____*The Famous Novelist*___		

Text the Child Is Reading	Line in the Text	Running Record
It was a dark and stormy night.	1	✓ ✓ d- d- dark ✓ ✓ ✓
The famous writer typed rapidly.	2	✓ fa- famous ✓ ✓ ✓ repeatedly
The words flowed like lightning.	3	
Suddenly, a shot rang out.	4	
Or so it seemed.	5	
The dog bowl flipped over in the wind.	6	
The neighborhood cat meowed.	7	
The famous writer stopped typing.	8	
He couldn't think of an ending.	9	
But he was hungry now.	10	

focuses more attention on oral reading performance. Some IRIs are more useful if comprehension is your priority, because of the age of your students and your need to identify texts at an appropriate level. Still other IRIs emphasize prior knowledge and attitudes toward reading. A few IRIs are specially designed for older adolescents and adults.

Administering an IRI requires spending some time with the manual of assessment procedures. Administering an IRI usually begins with making an educated guess about where to start: Make a guess about a student's approximate **independent reading level.** The independent level is where you believe the student reads with little difficulty and few errors. This is usually expressed in terms of grade level, such as the *third grade reading level* or the *eighth grade reading level.* Next, have the student read the graded word lists (lists of words grouped according to grade level) to follow up on your hunch and give you another rough idea about his or her reading level. Finally, have the student read a range of graded reading passages (passages arranged according to grade level, such as first grade, second grade, and so on), starting where you expect the reading to be easy and then progressing to more challenging texts (Paris and Carpenter 2003).

FIGURE 11.8   Commercially Available Informal Reading Inventories

Advanced Reading Inventory—Grades 7 through college. William C. Brown Publishers.

Analytical Reading Inventory—Grades 2 through 9. Charles E. Merrill Publishing Company.

Bader Reading and Language Inventory—Preprimer through twelfth grade reading levels. Macmillan Publishing Company.

Basic Reading Inventory—Preprimer through eighth grade levels. Kendall/Hunt Publishing Company.

Classroom Reading Inventory—Preprimer through eighth grade reading levels. McGraw-Hill.

Contemporary Classroom Reading Inventory—Grades 2 through 9. Gorsuch Scarisbrick Publishers.

Diagnostic Reading Inventory—Grades 3 through 8. Kendall/Hunt Publishing.

Ekwall/Shanker Reading Inventory—Preprimer through ninth grade reading levels. Allyn and Bacon.

Individual Evaluation Procedures in Reading—Primer through tenth grade levels. Prentice-Hall.

Informal Reading Assessment—Preprimer through twelfth grade reading levels. Rand McNally.

Informal Reading Inventory—Preprimer through twelfth grade. Houghton Mifflin.

Sucher–Allred Reading Placement Inventory—Primer through ninth grade reading levels. Available from Economy Publishing Company.

Qualitative Reading Inventory 3—Elementary grades through high school. Allyn and Bacon.

FIGURE 11.9   **Scoring Criteria for an Informal Reading Inventory**

For oral reading, based on miscues:

- **Easy:** a text that the student reads with 95 to 100 percent accuracy (sometimes called the **independent level**)
- **Instructional:** a text that the student reads with 90 to 94 percent accuracy
- **Difficult:** a text that the student reads with 89 percent or less accuracy (sometimes called the **frustration level**)

For comprehension, based on retelling score or correctly answered comprehension questions:

- **Easy:** 95 to 100 percent correct
- **Instructional:** 90 to 94 percent correct
- **Difficult:** below 89 percent or less correct

Informal reading inventories provide criteria, based on oral reading and comprehension performance, for deciding on the actual reading level. Oral reading performance usually involves a calculation of miscues. Comprehension performance is determined through retellings or comprehension questions. For retellings, a list of important facts and concepts is provided, and the examiner/teacher simply counts the number of facts and concepts that are mentioned in the student's retelling. Comprehension questions usually cover facts as well as interpretations and are calculated as the number correct. Figure 11.9 depicts one set of scoring criteria for determining a child's reading level on an informal reading inventory.

From these analyses, it becomes possible to recommend texts for instruction and for pleasure reading and also to understand when texts may be overly challenging. For instance, an IRI might indicate that a third grader should find third grade texts very easy to read, whereas fourth grade texts appear to be on his instructional level. Fifth grade texts might be too hard for him. Alternatively, an IRI might indicate that a second grader is likely to find second grade texts too difficult, whereas first grade texts should be more appropriate instructional texts. Teachers can make some useful instructional decisions on the basis of these benchmarks and can also use this information as a baseline from which to observe changes in development from later administrations of the IRI.

Be cautious, however, in applying these criteria. Although IRIs have been shown to correlate well with other widely accepted tests, such as the Gates–MacGinitie Reading Test, and they appear to be very reliable (Paris, Pearson, et al. 2002), they also have some limitations. IRIs can vary in difficulty, length, and familiarity with respect to your students, all of which variables can influence a child's reading and comprehension performance. Further, there may be differences in the retelling procedures and comprehension questions that can produce different results across IRIs. Especially with regard to considering reading level, always compare the results from IRIs with results from other measures, such as kidwatching, daily performance in the classroom, and high-stakes tests. Practice, dialogue with colleagues, and professional development can all help build your expertise in using IRIs (Lipson and Wixson 2003).

Content Area Reading Inventories

A content area literacy inventory (CARI) is especially useful when you want to see how a child naturally deals with school-based readings or assignments (Vacca and Vacca 2002). It is a particularly good tool to determine how older readers (upper elementary school students and adolescents) understand work and assessments in your class. A content area literacy inventory can incorporate many of the procedures discussed so far in the chapter—kidwatching, miscue inventory, informal reading inventory—but in the context of classroom texts and assignments.

To create a content area literacy inventory, follow these steps:

1. Select an assignment that you would like students to do. This can be just about anything, including reading pages from a book, doing math or science work, or studying pages from a social studies text.
2. Select a page or two at most from their work. Ask the child: *What do you need to do with this reading/assignment? How are you going to get started?*
3. Have the child read some of the reading/assignment orally. Watch for patterns in the child's reading, such as ability to read the words smoothly without disruption of the meaning. Ask: *What do you do when you come to something you do not know?*
4. Observe the child's use of text aids, such as graphs, problems, and questions inserted in the text. Most kids, particularly struggling readers, skip text aids. Some good readers skip text aids because they can get enough meaning from the rest of the text. Select a text aid, and ask the child to tell you what it is for and what it is telling him or her.
5. Ask the child to walk you through how she or he is going to approach the assignment. This step can be a little confusing to explain. Try saying "As you work on this, I want you to tell me how you are doing this." The result should be a think-aloud as the child completes the assignment.

Then, to evaluate the child's performance, follow these steps:

1. Observe problems with reading fluency. For instance, does the child demonstrate limited knowledge of sound–symbol relationships? Does the child skip or seriously alter words in ways that change or distort the meaning of the text?
2. Determine whether the child is more concerned with procedure (pronouncing the words, filling in blanks, and getting the assignment done) or is engaged in the content (talks about the content, asks questions about the content, and summarizes what she or he understands).

3. Watch for the child's ability to integrate text information. Less proficient readers often ignore large chunks of important text information and hence extract less meaning. Proficient readers make strategic use of all of the text information they need to comprehend well and complete assignments successfully. Sometimes, proficient readers skip text information because they figure out that it is not necessary for completing an assignment.

Portfolio Assessment

Simply defined, a **portfolio** is a gathering of students' work (Valencia 1990). A portfolio is a large, expandable file folder that holds

- samples of student work selected by the teacher or student
- a teacher's observations and notes
- a student's self-evaluation
- notes about a student's progress, contributed by the teacher and student

A goal in developing a portfolio is to gather a variety of indicators of learning so that teachers, administrators, students, and parents get the most comprehensive picture possible of a student's development.

There are a number of decisions to make if you choose to include portfolios as part of your approach to classroom assessment. First, think about your curriculum goals and your students. Ideally, portfolios should reflect development with respect to curriculum expectations and patterns of development appropriate for different age levels. Second, consider what you are doing in the classroom to help students meet curriculum goals. Your instruction should be consistent with your goals, and assessment should be consistent with your instruction.

After you have articulated the goals of using portfolios in your classroom, it is important to consider how to organize your students' portfolios. Portfolios typically consist of two parts: (1) evidence, work samples, or raw data that exemplify learning, and (2) summary sheets or an organizing framework that explains or helps synthesize the gathered work. Figure 11.10 depicts one portfolio entry.

The distinguishing strength of portfolios, in comparison with other assessments discussed so far, lies in their potential for student involvement. Students can get involved in selecting their work, organizing and interpreting it, and evaluating what they have accomplished. But we have to help students learn how to do these things. We need to model each behavior—selecting, organizing, interpreting, and evaluating—so that students can learn to do these things collaboratively with us, with each other, and on their own.

To initiate portfolios, some teachers bring in their own examples—portfolios containing family pictures, professional work, covers of favorite books, and the like. Explain to students the significance of items in your own portfolio so that they will get an idea of how portfolios uniquely portray things about individuals. In the

Cowboy Pete is asleep on his horse. His horse is named Flash because he runs fast. But not right now.

by Neil

Name........Neil................

Date ......1-26-03.................

Summary

I want to include this in my portfolio because:

I like this computer picture and how I made the words go with it.

FIGURE 11.10   A Sample Portfolio Entry

beginning, students will need lots of assistance selecting examples and explaining their selections. Continuous modeling of how to make choices and create explanations will help. Some teachers even construct mini-lessons about making selections and the various reasons for selections. (One of the simplest reasons is just selecting the best work.) Students can also choose something they have learned, especially something that took a long time, required a lot of effort, or involved interests outside of school. More sophisticated choices usually involve collaboration between teachers and students and focus on curriculum goals. These choices might focus on writing samples, results of content area tests, or student work samples, such as story maps, reader response, and class projects (Vizyak 1999).

Students also need help in evaluating their choices. One way to evaluate portfolios is through the idea of **quality work.** Most students are accustomed to simply handing things in and getting a score or a grade. To evaluate portfolios effectively, students need to understand what it means to produce quality work—in reading and writing performance and in response to classroom assignments and

FIGURE 11.11   Questions to Guide Student Reflection about Portfolios

What is your favorite piece (or the best piece) in your portfolio?

Why is this piece your favorite (or the best)?

Do you think your writing (or your reading, math, science, or social studies work) has improved? How?

How can you improve your writing (or your reading, math, science, or social studies work)?

How can teachers help you improve your writing (or your reading, math, science, or social studies work)?

projects. To help students develop this concept, teachers can adopt the practice of asking students this question with every assignment: *If we do quality work on this assignment, what will it look like?* Teachers and students can then discuss what it means to do the best work on an assignment, even participating in creating the evaluation criteria and grading scheme for the assignment. Figure 11.11 lists additional questions that are useful in helping students evaluate the contents of their portfolio.

It has become popular in recent years to engage students in using portfolios to evaluate their work during parent conferences. Remember to model each of the steps that students will need to know in order to do this. First, they will need to be intimately involved in making and explaining their own portfolio choices. Next, they need to have practice in evaluating and reflecting on their own work. Finally, organize and guide practice sessions for students so that they can converse comfortably with parents about what they have learned.

Interpreting Classroom Assessment Information

With so many teachers, schools, and districts engaged in gathering assessment information, a new problem has emerged: what to do with all of that assessment information. In recent years, I have encountered many teachers who are responsible each month for giving an entire battery of assessments—standardized tests, informal reading inventories, and classroom assessments for every subject. Their complaint is predictable and understandable: so much assessment and so little time for interpretation.

What's the answer? It starts with being careful about the number of assessments given and giving assessments for very specific purposes. Clearly defined purposes for assessment aid in interpretation. If you know exactly why you gave the test, chances are you know what you are looking for in student performance.

Beyond not giving so many tests in the first place, the next piece of advice is based on common sense: *Look for patterns in student performance.* Test makers and researchers call this **triangulation** (Glaser and Strauss 1967). Triangulation means viewing the same pattern of performance from the vantage points of different kinds of assessment. For example, you might observe that a child is experiencing difficulty with fluency during oral reading in your classroom. A follow-up informal reading inventory might show that the child is actually quite fluent. The conclusion, in this case, might be that reading aloud in class is a nerve-wracking experience even for this student, who really does not have a problem with fluency. Another child, who has difficulty with oral reading performance in class *and* on the informal reading inventory, might actually have a problem with reading fluency. Observing the same pattern of oral reading performance in two different assessment situations tends to confirm this conclusion.

Interpreting test information through such comparisons of performance patterns can be extremely important; it can refute some hunches about how students are doing and confirm others. There are many cases where students' classroom performance does not match up well with their performance on large-scale tests. Looking for patterns of performance can help unlock many of these kinds of assessment mysteries.

What to Do When Your Test Doesn't Work

Nearly every teacher has given a test on which all or nearly all students did poorly. Most of us know enough not to blame the students automatically, though there are cases where students simply are not prepared. Problems with tests can range from the extremely subtle to the glaringly obvious. Subtle problems often arise from the wording of questions. In many mathematics texts, questions are sometimes asked in a very truncated, abrupt fashion, such as: To the nearest, round 3.764. It should come as no surprise that many students find this kind of question difficult because they don't know what the question is asking. Sometimes, questions are asked in an incredibly convoluted manner, leaving students unable to organize for themselves an appropriate response. Other times, we innocently create test questions that—unbeknownst to us—are uninterpretable. But our students' poor performance can be an indicator of our own poorly constructed test.

If you have a hunch that a test is responsible for poor student performance, consider doing the following:

- Critically examine patterns of performance. If students fail to perform well in significant numbers on an item or two, or an entire test, take a careful look at your test and how students responded.
- Discuss with students how they went about answering test questions.
- Have students write questions that they think should be on a test you are about to give.
- Modify your grading appropriately if the test is at fault.

Redesigning Assessment on the Basis of What You Learn

The more we give classroom tests, the better we become at designing, giving, and interpreting tests—but only if we take the time and make the effort to modify our assessments in accordance with what we learn. We can learn some aspects of good test construction by revising our tests in response to what we see in the tests themselves. But the more powerful changes are often based on what we see our students doing with our tests. Use the ideas presented in this chapter to create your own ideal battery of tests, and compare your students' performance from a variety of perspectives, so that you can use classroom assessment to its fullest potential.

SPECIAL PROJECTS

For Beginning Teachers

Consider carefully the goals you will have with your students. Think about curriculum goals for the level you wish to teach, and consider what is appropriate for children at your grade level. Now think about the classroom tests described in this chapter. Select from among the tests described in this chapter and describe how you would develop your own approach to classroom assessment. What would this type of assessment look like to someone who came into your classroom?

For Experienced Teachers

Select one of the assessments described in this chapter—kidwatching, miscue analysis, running records, informal reading inventory, content area reading inventory, or portfolio assessment—and try it out in your classroom. Discuss your experiences with a colleague.

SUGGESTED READINGS

Barrentine, S. (1999). *Reading assessment: Principles and practices for elementary teachers.* Newark, DE: International Reading Association.

Hebert, E. (2001). *The Power of portfolios: What children can teach us about learning and assessment.* New York: Jossey-Bass.

Leslie, L., & Caldwell, J. (2001) *Informal reading inventory: III.* New York: Allyn and Bacon.

Mahoney, J. (2002). *Power and portfolios: Best practices for high school classrooms.* Portsmouth, NH: Heinemann.

Valencia, S., Hiebert, E., & Afflerbach, P. (1994). *Authentic reading assessment: Practices and possibilities.* Newark, DE: International Reading Association.

12 Communicating Assessment Information

How to improve communication about assessment with students, parents, and the school community

What's Really Going on Here?

Assessment seems to be particularly prone to miscommunication. Take, for example, what the media do with assessment information. State tests are commonly referred to as standardized when they are not, and student performance is simply compared from one year to the next when a whole host of factors may be involved—including a faulty test. When not engaged in communicating about tests in this way, the media are often in search of "feel-good" stories about students who have succeeded on a project or take an educational field trip. Between these extremes—test performance and the success-of-the-week stories—lies the story of what's really going on in student performance and achievement.

Another area ripe for miscommunication is communication with parents about assessment. Parents naturally want to know how their children are doing, especially that they are doing well. Most parents don't want to hear bad news. Some parents experienced their own difficulties as children at school and heard only bad news themselves throughout their school career. One of the most difficult things teachers do is to communicate when students are doing poorly. Although schools and districts do many things to communicate generally (letters home, bulletins, and so on), problems nearly always emerge with respect to communicating students' progress. A good measure of the problems can be attributed to failing to address the questions in which parents are most interested: What are you trying to accomplish with my child? How is my child doing? What are you doing to help my child? Responsible (and responsive) communication about assessment needs to address these questions directly.

With so much potential for miscommunication, educators need to take charge of communication about assessment. There are a multitude of stakeholders interested in assessment—students, parents, teacher-colleagues, administrators, and even yourself. A good assessment system communicates readily and effectively to each of these audiences. The following sections depict one school district's struggle with these issues and what to do about them.

The Case of Anytown School District

There is a school district that I know that has at least three distinct grading systems: one at the elementary level, another at the middle school level, and a third at the high school. In the description that follows, I will call this district Anytown District.

The Elementary Schools

In the elementary schools, the report card uses terms such as *Excellent, Satisfactory, Needs Improvement,* and *Unsatisfactory.* A sample report card is shown in Figure 12.1. Elementary schools appear to go out of their way to create grading systems that are not quantified. Instead, descriptive labels are used to describe the desired levels of achievement.

In the elementary schools in Anytown District, some teacher recently experimented with alternative formats for reporting students' progress. One such effort focused on making report card terminology more reflective of how children develop in their literacy: *Proficient, Progressing, Developing,* and *Emerging.* Still another effort tried to capture the stages that students go through as they develop proficiency in a particular area, such as reading fluency: *Alphabetic Knowledge, Phonemic Awareness, Word Recognition,* and *Oral Reading Fluency.* Despite these small efforts, the district's central office held firm on the report card format, arguing that it was familiar to parents.

Indeed, parents liked the familiar Excellent–Satisfactory–Needs Improvement–Unsatisfactory format. In fact, a frequent ritual was for parents to meet over the backyard fence and compare their children's performance:

"You know, my Erin got 9 E's on her last report card!"
"Is that so? Well, my Jason got 11 E's and no U's!"

FIGURE 12.1   A Sample Elementary School Report Card

	Excellent	Satisfactory	Needs Improvement	Unsatisfactory
Vocabulary study	√			
Story questions		√		
Writing practice		√		
Grammar practice			√	
Portfolio		√		
Reading informational materials			√	

Note that despite the fact that there were no numbers on the report cards, parents insisted on quantifying their children's' grades! What began as an attempt by the district to explain student performance was turned into an exercise in competition out in the community.

Some teachers tried out the alternative assessment labels during parent–teacher conferences. Simply changing the descriptive labels—from E's and U's to *Emergent* and *Proficient*—did not make things any better; many parents complained that they could not compare these new innovative labels with the traditional labels. Parents continuously exert tremendous pressure to keep the traditional reporting the same as it has always been.

The Middle Schools

There are two middle schools in Anytown School District. Report card practices shift dramatically, at the middle school level, to numerically based grades. The following scale depicts the range of possible scores for different grades:

Points	Grade
95–100	A+
90–94	A
85–89	B+
80–84	B
75–79	C+
70–74	C
65–69	D
64 and below	F

Students and their parents typically experience some initial discomfort with the new grading system. Several factors temper their discomfort, however. First, this system is familiar to the parents. It is what they experienced in high school. And it is easier than ever to compare one student's performance with that of another.

Second, teachers have developed a way for students to achieve at the highest levels even if they do not hand in their work in a timely manner. Most (if not all) teachers allow students to make up their work in the final week of each marking period. Their rationale: The transition from elementary to middle school can be daunting for kids, and they may need extra time to get their work done. The results of this practice are evident at the end of each marking period in terms of the high percentages of students on the A-honor roll. To get on the A-honor roll, students need to show an overall A-average for all of their classes. In each middle school, more than 70 percent of the student body regularly achieves this distinction. Students and their parents, especially in the upper echelons of achievement, are very happy with this system.

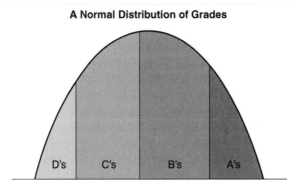

FIGURE 12.2   Anytown High School's Grading Patterns

The High School

Anytown High School continues the grading system used in the middle school but applies a very different set of grading practices. For instance, gone are the days of making up work in the final week of the marking period. Additionally, many teachers in the high school have great disdain for the generous grading at the middle school. They prefer to create a distribution of grades that looks more like a curve, with 20 percent or less of the students at the upper end with A's, 30 percent or so with B's, 30 percent with C's and 20 percent with D's and lower, as depicted in Figure 12.2.

A regular ritual at Anytown High School involves students coming up to teachers in the final week of the marking period and asking to make up their lost work, as they were able to do at the middle level. But the high school teachers do not allow make-ups. As a result, more and more students achieve at lower levels in high school than they did at the middle school. During parent conferences, long lines of parents wait to discuss why their child is not doing as well as in previous years. Some are quite concerned, even upset. The principal, accustomed to this ritual, backs up his teachers, saying, "We are tougher on the kids to help prepare them for college." Some parents buy it. Others are disgruntled. Still others try to find out what they can do to help their children do better.

What's Wrong with This Picture?

What's behind the roller coaster ride that students and their parents experience at Anytown School District? The first and most obvious problem is the failure to offer consistent messages about assessment throughout the system. Each level of the district has created its own culture of assessment on the basis of past practices, shared beliefs, and tradition. Communication about assessment—in the form of grading and reporting practices—can seem painfully arbitrary.

Second, not only are the messages different from one level to the next, but it is difficult for students and their parents to determine why and how a teacher arrived at a particular grade, whether it be an Emerging, an 87, or a B+. A built-in problem in any school-wide assessment system is developing language that actually means something. Note the absence of connections between grades and educational standards, between labels used for assessment (excellent, proficient, 92, or A) and classroom performance. In fact, in Anytown School District, it is not uncommon for students and parents to challenge a grade simply because connections between classroom performance and grading are unclear. Many students and their parents feel that assessment in Anytown is unfair, unless, of course, they are among the blessed majority of high performers at the middle school.

Fairness in assessment comes from striving to be clear and consistent in the messages given throughout the assessment system. Anytown School District is a case of miscommunication and mixed messages—a prime formula for generating feelings of unfairness. Moreover, without substantive feedback underlying the awarding of grades, students do not know how to get better and achieve at higher levels. Have you ever experienced a time when you were graded and had no idea how the grade was derived or what you could do to improve? Remember how helpless you felt? Anytown, and districts like it, could be much more productive if they adopted assessment practices based on clarity and consistency in what the assessment system communicates to all. The following sections outline practices that are the foundation of good communication about assessment.

Connect Assessment to Educational Standards

Conspicuously absent in the assessment information from Anytown is any reference to educational standards. Focusing instruction and assessment on standards could help redirect the assessment conversation toward what students are actually supposed to learn, how students are doing, and how teachers are helping them. Of course, this work starts by identifying and translating standards into commitments to practice. It is not uncommon for the conversation about standards to move directly to instruction, with no consideration of assessment. Include conversations about assessment and how to make assessment consistent with standards at all levels of the educational system.

Make Assessment Consistent with Instruction

Because assessment can be governed by tradition and custom, it is entirely possible to use assessment practices that are disconnected from instruction. Several examples illustrate this issue.

In the early grades, early reading fluency is an important goal. There are many different ways to assess reading fluency, from the use of standardized tests to informal reading inventories and classroom observations. For some children, fluency comes relatively easily: Their home environment and other aspects of their lives provide them with plenty of experience with language, experience that helps them translate their oral language proficiency into making key connections between oral language and print. Many other children require specific instruction in the foundations of fluency—awareness of the alphabet, sound–symbol relationships, and a sense of how consonants and vowels combine to make words.

Students who lack fluency lack the foundation they need in order to comprehend. Giving young students a reading comprehension test before they have achieved requisite levels of fluency wouldn't be very productive. As a result, the appropriate match between instruction in fluency and assessment is a test of fluency.

Teachers in the middle grades are often concerned with comprehension. The motto for teaching and learning in many subject areas is *teach for understanding*. This means students need to understand the concepts and relationships among concepts that make up knowledge in an area. Stated another way, it is not enough just to know the facts and be able to regurgitate them. Students need to understand themes, concepts, and relationships in deeper ways.

With this as a goal, there are many possible ways to assess students' knowledge. The pressures of large class sizes and limited time sometimes restrict the choices a teacher can make. For example, a teacher might choose to use a multiple-choice or true/false test rather than an essay test. Although it is possible to get at concepts and relationships using these formats, the information they provide is extremely limited. More important, concepts and relationships are more often assessed on large-scale tests using constructed-meaning, short-answer or extended-response question formats. Consequently, if teachers use only multiple-choice tests, students' understandings will be inadequately assessed *and* they will fail to gain valuable practice with testing formats, such as short-answer and essay questions, that are more in line with what they have learned.

Involve Students in Assessment

Ideally, students should be involved with assessment decisions early on and at every level of the educational system. A good way to do this is to work with the idea of quality work, introduced in Chapter 7 of this text. Whenever teachers give students an assignment or a task to complete, they should ask, "If you do a good job on this, how will you know? What will it look like?" Answering these questions can be difficult for students (and even adults) who are accustomed only to handing things in without worrying about quality. However, the answers to these questions provide a good foundation for helping students produce quality work, as well as encouraging students to work more directly on their own behalf toward higher levels of achievement.

Make the Assessments *Mean* Something

Many of us assess in ways that are practiced in Anytown, whether or not we wish to acknowledge it. This often means we adopt the arbitrariness of the assessment systems passed down to us by others.

Why is a 65 or lower considered a failing grade? Why is the failing point a 60 to others? How about a 55? Or a 30? Why is a 95 a good grade? The answer to these questions is that we arbitrarily conspire with one another to give these numbers meaning. For the same reason, the system of E's, U's, and so on at the elementary level persists.

It is usually difficult, both in school and out of school, to have conversations about the meaning behind different assessment practices, yet it is absolutely vital. Resistance to doing this often comes from a sense of competitiveness about our assessment practices ("He grades harder than I do") or from our own collective awareness that few of us have ever been taught how to assess. Rarer still are opportunities to talk about assessment in a nonthreatening atmosphere.

Throughout the educational system, assessment numbers and labels take on meaning only as each individual teacher makes them mean something. Confusion emerges when the numbers and labels tend to mean too many things or when it is impossible for students and parents to tell whether they mean anything at all. To confront this challenge, educators need to talk collectively about the meaning(s) behind their assessment practices. Not everyone needs to assess in identical ways. However, there can be considerable benefits in clarity and fairness for everyone if educators can reach some agreement with regard to the meanings and messages underlying our assessment practices.

Communicate, Communicate, Communicate!

This final principle would go a long way toward resolving Anytown School District's problems with assessment. One can only wonder what would happen if the district developed an ongoing conversation about teaching and learning, with assessment at the center. What would happen if this conversation were part of everyday communication with students? What would happen if parents were brought into the conversation, rather than standing outside looking in and wondering what to make of the district's assessment practices? One answer to these questions is that everyone—teachers, administrators, students, and their parents—would have a better idea of what they were working toward with respect to teaching and learning and how to help students succeed. Working with others in your educational system, and communicating freely and often, may you find success in creating an ongoing assessment conversation for you and your students.

SPECIAL PROJECTS

For Beginning Teachers

Make some recommendations for Anytown School District. What could or should the district do to improve communication about assessment?

For Experienced Teachers

Compare the assessment challenges of Anytown School District with the assessment practices in your school or district. What ways could you improve communication? Now take a hard look at your own assessment practices. In what ways could you improve communication? For your students? For parents? For colleagues?

SUGGESTED READINGS

Gusky, T., & Bailey, J. (2000). *Developing grading and reporting systems for student learning.* Thousand Oaks, CA: Corwin Press.

Marzano, T. (2000). *Transforming classroom grading.* Alexandria, VA: Association for Supervision and Curriculum Development.

Stiggins, R. (2005). *Student involved classroom assessment for learning.* Columbus, OH: Prentice-Hall. See especially the chapter on communicating assessment information.

APPENDIX A

State Department of Education Websites

Alabama
www.alsde.edu

Alaska
www.educ.state.ak.us

Arizona
www.ade.state.az.us

California
www.cde.ca.gov

Colorado
www.cde.state.co.us

Connecticut
www.state.ct.us/sde

Delaware
www.doe.state.de.us

Florida
www.fldoe.org

Georgia
www.doe.k12.ga.us

Hawaii
www.doe.k12.hi.us/

Idaho
www.sde.state.id.us/Dept/

Illinois
www.isbe.state.il.us

Indiana
www.doe.state.in.us/

Iowa
www.state.ia.us/educate/

Kansas
www.ksbe.state.ks.us/

Kentucky
www.education.ky.gov/

Louisiana
www.doe.state.la.us/Ide

Maine
www.state.me.us/education/
homepage.htm

Maryland
www.msde.state.md.us/

Massachusetts
www.doe.mass.edu/

Michigan
www.michigan.gov/mde

Minnesota
www.education.state.mn.us/html/
mde_home.htm

Mississippi
www.mde.k12.ms.us/

Missouri
www.dese.state.mo.us/

Montana
www.opi.state.mt.us/index.html

Nebraska
www.nde.state.ne.us

Nevada
www.nde.state.nv.us

New Hampshire
www.ed.state.nh.us/

New Jersey
www.state.nj.us/education/

New Mexico
www.sde.state.nm.us

New York
www.nysed.gov/

North Carolina
www.ncpublicschools.org/

North Dakota
www.dpi.state.nd.us/

Ohio
www.ode.state.oh.us

Oklahoma
www.sde.state.ok.us/

Oregon
www.ode.state.or.us/

Pennsylvania
www.pde.psu.edu

Rhode Island
www.ridoe.net/

South Carolina
www.sde.state.sc.us/sde/

South Dakota
www.state.sd.us/deca/

Tennessee
www.state.tn.us/education/

Texas
www.tea.state.tx.us/

Utah
www.usoe.k12.ut.us

Vermont
www.state.vt.us/educ/

Virginia
www.pen.k12.va.us/

Washington
www.k12.wa.us/

West Virginia
http://wvde.state.wv.us

Wisconsin
www.dpi.state.wi.us

Wyoming
www.k12.wy.us

Yopp–Singer Test of Phonemic Segmentation

Directions for Administering

- Have one test sheet for each child in the class.
- Assess children individually in a quiet place.
- Keep the assessment playful and gamelike.
- Explain the game to the child exactly as the directions specify.
- Model for the child what he or she needs to do with each of the practice words. Have the children break apart each word with you.

Instructions

Children are given the following directions upon administration of the test:

Today we're going to play a word game. I'm going to say a word and I want you to break the word apart. You are going to say the word slowly, and then tell me each sound in the word in order. For example, if I say "old," you should say "oooo-llll-d." [the teacher says the sound, not the letters]. Let's try a few words together.

The practice items are *ride, go,* and *man.* The teacher should help the child with each sample item, segmenting the item for the child if necessary and encouraging the child to repeat the segmented words. Then the child is given the 22-item test. If the child responds correctly, the teacher says, "That's right." If the child gives an incorrect response, he or she is corrected. The teacher provides the appropriate response. The teacher circles the numbers of all correct answers. If the child breaks a word apart incorrectly, the teacher gives the correct answer:

	Child says	You say
Uses onset and rime	/d/-/og/	/d-/o-/g/
Repeats word	dog	/d-/o-/g/
Stretches word out	d-o-g	/d-/o-/g/
Spells letters in word	"d"-"o"-"g"	/d-/o-/g/
Says first and last sounds	/d/-/g/	/d-/o-/g/
Says another word	bark	/d-/o-/g/
Says a sentence	I don't know	/d-/o-/g/

Scoring

The child's score is the number of items correctly segmented into all constituent phonemes. No partial credit is given. For instance, if a child says "/c/-/at/" instead of "/c/-/a/-/t/," the response may be noted on the blank line following the items but is considered incorrect for purposes of scoring. Correct responses are only those that involve articulation of each phoneme in the target word.

A blend contains two or three phonemes in each of these and each should be articulated separately. Hence, item 7 on the test, *grew,* has three phonemes, /g/-/r/-/ew/. Digraphs such as /sh/ in item 5, *she,* and the /th/ in item 15, *three,* are single phonemes. Item 5 therefore has two phonemes, and item 15 has three phonemes. If a child responds with letter names instead of sounds, the response is coded as incorrect, and the type of error is noted on the test.

Students who obtain high scores (segmenting all or nearly all of the items correctly) may be considered phonemically aware. Students who correctly segment some items are displaying emerging phonemic awareness. Students who are able to segment only a few items or none at all lack appropriate levels of phonemic awareness. Without intervention, those students who score very low on the test are likely to experience difficulty with reading and spelling.

Student Test Sheet

Yopp–Singer Test of Phoneme Segmentation

Student's name _____ Date _____

Score (number correct) _____

Directions: "Today we're going to play a word game. I'm going to say a word and I want you to break the word apart. You are going to tell me each sound in the word in order. For example, if I say "old," you should say /o/-/l/-/d/. Let's try a few together."

(Administrator: Be sure to say the sounds, not the letters, in the word.)

Practice items: (Assist the child in segmenting these items as necessary.)

ride   **go**   **man**

Test items: (Circle those items that the student correctly segments; incorrect responses may be recorded on the blank line following the item.)

1. dog _____	**12.** lay _____
2. keep _____	**13.** race _____
3. fine _____	**14.** zoo _____
4. no _____	**15.** three _____
5. she_____	**16.** job _____
6. wave_____	**17.** in _____
7. grew _____	**18.** ice _____
8. that _____	**19.** at _____
9. red_____	**20.** top _____
10. me_____	**21.** by_____
11. sat _____	**22.** do_____

REFERENCES

Allington, R. (2002). *Big brother and the national reading curriculum: How ideology trumped evidence.* Portsmouth, NH: Heinemann.

Alvermann, D. E. (2001). *Effective literacy instruction for adolescents.* Chicago: National Reading Conference.

Amrein, A., & Berliner, D. (2002). "High-stakes testing, uncertainty, and student learning." *Education Evaluation and Policy Analysis Archives (Online Serial)* **10**(18). Retrieved January 12, 2003, from http://epaa.asu.edu/epaa/v10n18

Anderson, R., Hiebert, E., et al. (1985). *Becoming a nation of readers.* Champaign, IL: Center for the Study of Reading.

Armbruster, B., Lehr, F., et al. (2002). *A child becomes a reader: Birth to4 preschool.* Portsmouth, NH: RMC Research Corporation.

Bedrova, E., Leong, D., et al. (2000). A framework for early literacy instruction. Aurora, CO: Mid-continent Research for Education and Learning.

Berliner, D. (1996). *The manufactured crisis: Myths, fraud, and the attack on America's public schools.* New York: Perseus.

Brown, J., Goodman, Y., et al. (1996). *Studies in miscue analysis: An annotated bibliography.* Newark, DE: International Reading Association.

Bush, G. (2001). *No child left behind: Executive summary.* Washington, DC: U.S. Department of Education.

Clay, M. (1972). *The early detection of reading difficulties.* Portsmouth, NH: Heinemann.

Clay, M. (1993). *An observation survey.* Portsmouth, NH: Heinemann.

Conley, M. (1995). *Content reading instruction: A communication approach.* New York: McGraw-Hill.

Conley, M. (2001). *Identifying the mental models underlying state proficiency tests: When teaching to the test means responsible literacy practices.* San Antonio, TX: National Reading Conference.

Cooper, J., & Pikulski, J. (1999). *Do you believe this? Level 5.* New York: Houghton Mifflin.

Cunningham, P. (1999). *Phonics they use.* Upper Saddle River, NJ: Pearson.

Fine, B. (1947). *Our children are cheated: The crisis of American education.* New York: Holt.

Glaser, B., & Strauss, A., (1967). *Discovery of grounded theory: Strategies for qualitative research.* Amsterdam: Aldine de Gruyter.

Goodman, K. (1969). "Analysis of oral reading miscues: Applied psycholinguistics." *Reading Research Quarterly* **5:** 9–13.

Goodman, K., & Burke, C. (1972). *Reading miscue inventory: Procedure for diagnosis and correction.* New York: Macmillan.

Goodman, Y. (1999). Revaluing readers while readers revalue themselves: Retrospective miscue analysis. In *Reading assessment: Principles and practices for elementary teachers,* ed. S. Berrentine. Newark, DE: International Reading Association, pp. 140–151.

Goodman, Y. (2002). *Kidwatching: Documenting children's literacy development.* Portsmouth, NH: Heinemann.

Hoffman, J., & Crone, S. (1985). The oral recitation lesson: A research-derived strategy for reading in basal texts. In *Issues in literacy: A research perspective,* ed. J. Niles and R. Lalik. Rochester, NY: The National Reading Conference. 76–83.

Johnson, M., Kress, R., et al. (1987). *Informal reading inventories.* Newark, DE: International Reading Association.

Leslie, L., & Jett-Simpson, M. (1997). *Authentic literacy assessment: An ecological approach.* New York: Addison Wesley.

Lipson, M., & Wixson, K. (2003). *Assessment and instruction of reading and writing difficulty.* Boston: Allyn & Bacon.

Mazzeo, C. (2001). "Frameworks of state: Assessment policy in historical perspective." *Teachers College Record* **103**(3): 367–397.

McGraw-Hill, C. (2003). *Glossary of assessment terms.* Monterey, CA: CTB/McGraw-Hill.

National Center for Education Statistics. (1999). *Highlights from TIMMS: Overview and key findings.* Washington, DC: Office of Educational Research and Improvement, U.S. Department of Education.

National Commission on Excellence in Education. (1983). *A nation at risk: The imperative for educational reform.* Washington, DC: U.S. Department of Education.

National Reading Panel. (2000). *Report of the National Reading Panel: An evidence-based assessment of the scientific research literature on reading and its implications for reading instruction.* Washington, DC: National Institute of Child Health and Human Development, National Institutes of Health.

Neuman, S. (1998). *How can we enable all children to achieve?* Newark, DE: International Reading Association.

North Central Regional Educational Laboratory. (2003). *Using instructional assessments in the Reading First program.* **2003.** Naperville, IL: North Central Regional Educational Laboratory.

Ogle, D. (1986). "A Teaching model that develops active reading of expository text." *The Reading Teacher* **39**: 564–570.

Ohanian, S. (1999). *One size fits few: The folly of educational standards.* Portsmouth, NH: Heinemann.

Oxenbury, H. (1997). *The three little wolves and the big bad pig.* New York, Simon and Schuster.

Paris, S., & Carpenter, R. (2003). "FAQ's about IRI's." *The Reading Teacher* **56**(6): 578–580.

Paris, S., Pearson, P. D., et al. (2002). *Evaluation of the Michigan Literacy Progress Profile. Final Report. Year 1.* Lansing, MI: Department of Education.

Peterson, P. (2003). *Our schools and our future: Are we still at risk?* Washington, DC: Hoover Institution Press.

Popham, W. (2001). *Classroom assessment: What teachers need to know.* New York: Allyn & Bacon.

Popham, W. (2003). "The seductive allure of data." *Educational Leadership* **60**(5): 48–51.

Rasinski, T., & Hoffman, J. (2003). "Oral reading in the school literacy curriculum." *Reading Research Quarterly* **38**(4): 510–522.

Reutzel, R., Camperell, K., et al. (2002). Hitting the wall: Helping struggling readers comprehend. In *Improving comprehension instruction: Rethinking research, theory, and classroom practice,* ed. K. Block, L. Gambrell, and M. Pressley. San Francisco: Jossey-Bass, pp. 321–353.

Scieszka, J. (1996). *The true story of the three little pigs.* New York: Puffin Books.

Snow, C., Burns, S., et al. (1998). *Preventing reading difficulties in young children.* Washington, DC: National Academy Press.

Stahl, S., & Heuback, K. (in press). "Fluency-oriented reading instruction." *Elementary School Journal.*

Stevens, G., & DeBord, K. (2001). "Issues of assessment in testing children under the age of eight." *The Forum* **6**: 3.

Stiggins, R. (2002). "Assessment crisis: The absence of assessment FOR learning." *Phi Delta Kappan* **83**(10): 758–765.

Stiggins, R. (2005). *Student-centered classroom assessment for learning.* Columbus, OH: Prentice-Hall.

Vacca, R., & Vacca, J. (2002). *Content area reading: Literacy and learning across the curriculum.* New York: Addison-Wesley.

Valencia, S. (1990). "A portfolio approach to classroom reading assessment: The whys, whats, and hows." *The Reading Teacher* **43**(4): 338–340.

Valencia, S., & Wixson, K. (1999). *Policy-oriented research on literacy standards and assessment.* Ann Arbor: University of Michigan.

Vizyak, L. (1999). Student portfolios: Building self-reflection in a first-grade classroom. In *Reading assessment: Principles and practices for elementary teachers,* ed. S. Berrentine. Newark, DE: International Reading Association, pp. 135–139.

Wiggins, G. (1998). *Educative assessment.* San Francisco: Jossey-Bass.

Worthy, J., & Broaddus, K. (2002). "Fluency beyond the primary grades: From group performance to silent, independent reading." *The Reading Teacher* **55**(4): 334–343.

INDEX